AF353479

Shame, heritage affect support-seeking

Elizabeth T. Allen

TABLE OF CONTENT

ABSTRACT

Survivors of intimate partner violence (IPV) often face many barriers to help-seeking. Shame is a common emotion for IPV survivors and can hinder their desire to seek help, yet little is known about how racial-ethnic heritage and the experience of shame affects help-seeking desires. The aims of the current study were to (1) determine if survivors from different racialethnic heritage backgrounds will experience higher levels of shame than others, (2) examine the relationship between shame and use of formal and informal support systems, and (3) determine whether the relationship between shame and help-seeking differs among survivors of different racial-ethnic backgrounds. To address these aims, we analyzed secondary data from IPV survivors ($n = 193$) who completed an online questionnaire about relationship abuse. A one-way ANOVA proved that there were no significant racial-ethnic heritage differences in average levels of shame, however, ethnic differences were detected in three of the individual items in the shame scale. Results from three separate moderated logistic regressions indicated that there were no significant main effects between shame and help-seeking for formal, informal, or use of any help-seeking outlets, however, a significant interaction was observed between shame and racialethnic heritage for women of Korean racial-ethnic heritage on formal help-seeking desires. The interaction found that there was a positive relationship between shame and help-seeking for survivors of Korean descent, but shame was unrelated to help-seeking for other racial-ethnic heritages. Findings from this study have the possibility of informing and improving individual care programs for survivors that integrate a person's racial-ethnic heritage while including emotions into care plans to decrease survivor shame. Additionally, this study can inform formal and informal help-seeking providers about various barriers, like shame and racial-ethnic cultural beliefs, that a survivor of interpersonal violence may face.

ACKNOWLEDGMENTS

First and foremost, I would like to thank my mentor and book committee chair, Dr. Courtney Ahrens, for her patience and support throughout this whole process. I am grateful for the hours of discussion, teaching, and exploring we did not only on this project but also in the professional world. Next, I would like to thank Dr. May Ling Halim for her input and guidance in and out of the classroom. Also, I would like to thank Dr. Shelley Eriksen for her unwavering support of me as an academic and as a young professional, I will always be grateful for Not Alone @ the Beach. Finally, I would like to dedicate this book to my mother, Beverly. I am the woman I am because of the sacrifices that you made for our family; I know that Dad is proud of the both of us.

CHAPTER 1

INTRODUCTION

Intimate partner violence (IPV) against women is unfortunately all too common in today's society (Black et al., 2011; Breiding et al., 2014, Devries et al., 2013; Ellsberg et al., 2008; R. S. Thompson et al., 2006; Tjaden & Thonennes, 2000). IPV is defined as any violent act perpetrated by a past or present intimate partner (Kramer et al., 2004; Rennison & Welchans, 2000). This violent act can include many different forms of violence like stalking, sexual abuse, physical harm, emotional abuse, and more (Cho et al., 2020; Kramer et al., 2004; World Health Organization & Pan American Health Organization, 2012). In the United States, around 30% of female-identified survivors (Black et al., 2011; J. C. Campbell, 2002) and anywhere from 11%28% of male-identified individuals (Black et al., 2011; Goldberg & Meyer, 2013) have reported experiencing violence by a partner during their life. Prior literature estimated that at least 75% of female-identified folks seek some type of informal or formal help after experiencing violence (Edwards et al., 2012; Mahlstedt & Keeny, 1993). Even with high rates of help-seeking, helpseeking is particularly low among survivors of color who are less likely to seek-help than their White counterparts (Henning & Klesges, 2002; Kaukinen, 2004; Satyen et al., 2019).

Survivors of IPV are at risk of ongoing and escalating violence that can eventually put their lives and mental health at a costly risk if they do not seek help (Beck et al., 2015; Wisner et al., 1999). Studies have shown that survivors of IPV are at an elevated risk of long-term health consequences like chronic stress, risky health behaviors, and untreated injuries (Beck et al., 2015; Breiding et al., 2008; J. C. Campbell, 2002; Coker et al., 2002), which consequently cost the medical system over $8.3 billion (Max et al., 2004). There is also a wide array of negative outcomes for survivors who do not seek help at all like post-traumatic stress disorder (PTSD), depression, and other mental health related issues (Liang et al., 2005; Martin et al., 2008; Rodríguez et al., 2009). Specifically, minority women are at a higher risk of mental health issues associated with IPV (Rodríguez et al., 2009) and are less likely to utilize mental health professionals (Bent-Goodley, 2007). Understanding the barriers to help-seeking is thus a critical first step to helping survivors break their silence and disrupt the cycle of violence.

There are many factors that make it difficult for IPV survivors to seek help such as fear and lack of social support (Overstreet & Quinn, 2013), isolation (Lanier & Maume, 2009), shame (Kennedy & Prock, 2018; McCleary-Sills et al., 2016), race (Lipsky et al., 2006), and ethnicity (Liang et al., 2005). While internalized barriers such as shame have received a lot of theoretical attention, there has been surprisingly little empirical examination of the role that shame plays in IPV survivors' help-seeking decisions within diverse populations. There has also been a lack of research examining the role racial-ethnic heritage plays in the relationship between shame and help-seeking. The term racial-ethnic identity refers to the meaning and significance of race and ethnicity to a person's sense of self that focuses on cultural group membership (Oyserman et al., 2003; Sellers et al., 2006). For the purpose of this study, we will utilize the term *racial-ethnic* to describe a person's identity. To fill this gap in the literature around racial-ethnic differences, the current study will examine the relationship between shame and help-seeking among IPV survivors from different racial-ethnic backgrounds.

Prevalence of Intimate Partner Violence (IPV)

Research focusing on sexual orientation estimates that 35% of heterosexual women experience violence by an intimate partner at some point in their lifetime including 43.8% of lesbian women, 61.1% of bisexual women, 26% of gay men, 37.3% bisexual men, and 29% of heterosexual men (Walters et al., 2013). Transgender individuals experience a higher level of IPV prevalence (31.1%) than their cisgender peers (20.4%; Langenderfer-Magruder et al., 2016). Similarly, racial-ethnic differences have been found for IPV victimization among femaleidentified survivors, with Black women victimized at the highest rate (17.3%), followed by Latinas (15.2%), White (15.2%), and Asian women (10.3%; Cho, 2012). This study will focus on IPV among female identified survivors of Mexican, Korean, Vietnamese, and European (White) heritages.

Help-Seeking Among IPV Survivors

Although definitions of help-seeking vary (Rickwood & Thomas, 2012), help-seeking for the purpose of this study refers to the solicitation of any IPV assistance from either informal or formal support systems outside of oneself (Cornally & McCarthy, 2011; Overstreet & Quinn, 2013). There are three proposed stages for this process: (1) defining the problem, (2) deciding to seek help, and (3) choosing a path (e.g., seeking help from formal or informal sources; Liang et al., 2005). With this approach in mind, once survivors define the problem and decide to look for help, they are faced with two help-seeking options: formal or informal help. The decision to seek help does not always happen in a linear fashion and can adapt and change over time with the introduction of new information and feelings (Latta & Goodman, 2011). Prior literature highlights that there are many different paths a survivor can utilize to seek help after experiencing abuse (Breiding et al., 2014; Kaukinen, 2004; Sabina & Ho, 2014); however, when disclosing violence, IPV survivors are most likely to seek help from informal sources such as friends and family and are least likely to seek help from formal systems like the criminal justice system (Goodkind et al., 2003; McCart et al., 2010; Sylaska & Edwards, 2014). Factors like the fear of rejection, shame, cultural stigma, and societal pressures can lead to a lack of support from others which can cause disclosures of IPV to be infrequent or not disclosed at all (Deitz et al., 2015; Ullman, 1996; Walters, 2011). Even though IPV survivors are more likely to seek help from people close to them, overall disclosures of IPV remain low. Together, these findings highlight differences in IPV survivors' decisions to seek help from formal and informal support providers.

Formal Help-Seeking

Of those survivors who do seek formal help, formal help-seeking can be broadly defined as seeking help from a broad range of service providers including legal services, police, health services, medical personnel, shelters, and violence education outlets (Breiding et al., 2014; Duterte et al., 2008; Fugate et al., 2005; Kaukinen, 2004; Macy et al., 2005; Robinson et al., 2021). Studies show that less than half (36.5%-47.2%) of survivors seek help from health professionals (Ansara & Hindin, 2010; Breiding et al., 2014),

and less than 40% of IPV survivors seek help from the police or other criminal

justice personnel (Breiding et al., 2014; Kaukinen,

2004). Altogether, research shows the reporting to police is alarming low (Edwards

et al., 2012; Kaukinen, 2004). One potential reason for such low reporting is that

some survivors fear possible legal repercussions if they report to police or that prior

negative experiences with law enforcement scared them away from wanting to

report new experiences of violence (Fugate et al., 2005; Wolf et al., 2003). This

lack of formal help-seeking highlights the disconnect between survivor support and

resources available, especially since police personnel can provide formal resources

such as restraining orders and abuse documentation for protection from further

abuse

(Xie & Lynch, 2017; Wolf et al., 2003).

Not only is help-seeking from law enforcement low, but research also

suggests that seeking help from medical providers is low. Less than one third of

survivors report their experiences to medical care providers (Breiding et al., 2014;

Du Mont et al., 2005; Kaukinen, 2004), despite healthcare workers' ability to treat

physical injuries (Reisenhofer & Seibold, 2013). Medical service providers such as

nurses and doctors can help diagnose, treat, and manage acute injuries and chronic

health conditions resulting from IPV (J. C. Campbell, 2002; Reisenhofer & Seibold,

2013), yet medical help-seeking is not utilized and remains low (Duterte et al.,

2008; Kaukinen, 2004). Even though medical and social services are available for

survivors, less than half of survivors seek help from medical professionals, counselors, mental health professionals, or social service agencies (Kaukinen, 2004; Vranda et al., 2018). Survivors who do seek help from formal entities are most likely to report sexual or physical violence which can have long-lasting effects on the survivor's health (Coker et al., 2002; Duterte et al., 2008). Such low rates of reporting may be affected by a lack of systematic screening for IPV within the clinic or hospital (Chapin et al., 2011; Trevillion et al., 2014; Waalen et al., 2000). Other formal help-seeking routes, like crisis centers, yield even fewer disclosures of IPV.

Under 20% of survivors report their experience of violence to a crisis center (Du Mont et al.,

2005), despite crisis centers' ability to provide shelter, counseling, case management, employment assistance, and a wide range of other needed services (Sullivan, 2018; K. S. Wilson et al., 2007). College students might also look to a professional advocate employed through their university for resources available on and off campus (Carmody et al., 2009). As severity of violence increases, survivors of violence are more likely to utilize crisis centers and formal support systems, but many still do not seek professional or formal support systems (Ansara & Hindin, 2010; Coker et al., 2000). Such services are fairly widespread (Kulkarni, 2019), yet few IPV survivors engage these services, suggesting that personal and systemic barriers may be making it difficult for survivors to seek help. Together, these findings not only reveal a large deficit in formal reporting but also a large need to better understand how to meet the needs of all survivors at these formal institutions.

Informal Help-Seeking

While formal help-seeking opportunities might not be utilized by IPV survivors, seeking help from informal support providers like friends and family is another support opportunity for survivors. Family and friends are the most common type of informal support networks utilized by survivors looking for help (Ahrens & Campbell, 2000; Ansara & Hindin, 2010; Breiding et al., 2014; Dunham & Senn, 2000; Goodkind et al., 2003; Ingram, 2007; Kaukinen, 2004; McCart et al., 2010; Sylaska & Edwards, 2014; Ullman, 1996). These informal support networks are often the first point of contact and the most commonly used help-seeking source for survivors of IPV (Edwards et al., 2012; Sabina & Ho, 2014). Literature shows that most survivors choose to look for help from a comfortable source like a friend or family member as opposed to an unfamiliar person (Ansara & Hindin, 2010; Breiding et al., 2014; Dunham & Senn, 2000; Fanslow & Robinson, 2010). Surveys suggest that around half of survivors received help from their family (Breiding et al., 2014; Kaukinen, 2004) and 70% disclose to friends (Breiding et al., 2014). Overwhelmingly, studies show that friends receive the most disclosures (Barrett & Pierre, 2011; Coker et al., 2000; Edwards et al., 2012; Fisher et al., 2003; Mahlstedt & Keeny, 1993). Overall, literature supports the fact that survivors are more likely to disclose to a friend, family member, neighbor, coworker, and other informal sources before looking for formal help (Breiding et al., 2014; Sylaska & Edwards, 2014).

Informal support services vary in their ability to support a survivor. Factors like the informal support person's positive or negative reactions to learning about a violent experience (Sylaska & Edwards, 2014) and cultural beliefs around rape-myth acceptance (Paul et al., 2009) are all components that affect a survivor's quality of informal support. Yet even though informal support systems are more utilized than others, not all survivors disclose to friends and family and there are many barriers put in place that make it difficult for survivors to disclose to anyone.

Barriers to IPV Survivors' Help-Seeking

Survivors of IPV face many barriers to help-seeking; these barriers can be both internal and external. Barriers like family safety, personal beliefs, legal issues, and sociocultural factors are just a few barriers that survivors can experience (Dunlop et al., 2005; Hien & Ruglass, 2009; Robinson et al., 2021; Rodríguez et al., 2009). Prior literature states that both intrapersonal and interpersonal barriers may make it difficult for survivors to seek help and tell others about their experiences (Lelaurain et al., 2017; Lutenbacher et al., 2003; Simmons et al., 2015). Overstreet and Quinn (2013) proposed an intimate partner violence stigmatization model that highlights three barriers to help-seeking: internal, cultural, and anticipated stigma. Each of these barriers is described in more detail below.

Intrapersonal Barriers

Intrapersonal barriers are internal struggles or issues that hinder a person's desire to seek help. Overstreet and Quinn (2013) identify two key intrapersonal barriers: survivors' feelings and the meaning survivors attached to the violence

(Overstreet & Quinn, 2013; Sylaska & Edwards, 2014). The first intrapersonal barrier to help-seeking are survivors' feelings; these feelings can encompass a vast array of emotions which greatly affect a survivor's experiences after violence. Internal feelings of shame, hopelessness, embarrassment, and fear can cause a survivor to not seek-help (Beaulaurier et al., 2005; Fugate et al., 2005; Murray et al., 2018). Shame can lead to less help-seeking by making the survivor believe they deserved the abuse, that the abuse brings disgrace upon themselves and their family, and that if the survivor asks for help, it shows weakness and makes private problems public (Harrison & Esqueda, 1999; McClearySills et al., 2016; Morgan et al., 2016). Emotions can then, in turn, affect how survivors perceive their personal experience and become an intrapersonal barrier to help-seeking (Overstreet & Quinn, 2013).

The second intrapersonal barrier to help-seeking is the meaning that a survivor attaches to an assault (Sylaska & Edwards, 2014). The meaning and appraisal of IPV can differ from survivor to survivor. Some survivors of IPV do not associate themselves with the label of

"survivor" or "victim," proving how the lexical codes survivors use can vary and so can the meaning attached to the violent event (Liang et al., 2005; Orchowski et al., 2013; Simmons et al.,

2015). The survivor could also have different goals such as protecting the abuser (McLeod et al., 2010) or protecting themselves from further pain (Dienemann et al., 2005) by not disclosing. While these intrapersonal barriers certainly affect help-seeking decisions, external factors also can be a barrier for survivors.

Interpersonal Barriers

Interpersonal barriers are any barrier a survivor faces that happens outside of the individual. According to the intimate partner violence stigmatization model (Overstreet & Quinn,

2013), interpersonal barriers include cultural barriers and anticipated stigma.

The first interpersonal barrier to help-seeking involves culture. There are many helpseeking barriers put in place by culture like cultural norms around abuse and help-seeking, racism, sexism, lack of accessibility to services based off of culture, socioeconomic class, language barriers, and many more. Culture does not look or act one specific way, it varies depending on a person's racial-ethnic heritage, family, and how a person was raised. Survivors can experience a myriad of reactions when disclosing IPV. Victim-blaming is one of the most common social reactions that is imbedded within cultural understanding and acceptance of helpseeking. Victim-blaming includes accepted cultural statements or norms that place the punishment on the survivor for actions inflicted on them by another human being (Grubb & Turner, 2012; Whatley, 1996). These are often deleterious and can cause a survivor to receive negative reactions from people within their culture (Capezza & Arriaga, 2008; Hayes et al., 2013; Overstreet & Quinn, 2013; Rollero & De Piccoli, 2020; Rollero & Tartaglia, 2019; Sylaska & Edwards, 2014). Myths about intimate partner violence (e.g., women ask to be assaulted, victims lie about their assaults, the problem at hand is not a big issue) serve to devalue and minimize survivors' experience (Deitz et al., 2015; Edwards et al., 2011; Edwards et al.,

2012; Sylaska & Edwards, 2014). This can make it difficult for survivors to reach out for help. Gender also plays a role in victim-blaming. Women are more likely to get blamed for IPV because of their gender (Deitz et al., 2015; Edwards et al., 2012; Flood & Pease, 2009; Kennedy & Prock, 2018). Those who are affected by cultural myths will often be unwilling to seek support.

The final help-seeking barrier described by the intimate partner violence stigmatization model is anticipated stigma. Anticipated stigma is defined as, "expectations that others will react in stigmatizing ways if they find out about a stigmatizing identity, anticipated stigma refers to people's belief that others will discriminate against or socially reject them" (Murray et al., 2018, p. 6). Due to the fear of social rejection and anticipated stigma, survivors often look for help in indirect ways, like not explicitly saying that they are experiencing violence but instead saying that someone else is experiencing violence, which can lead to unsupportive network responses that further survivors' feelings of stigmatization when they disclose to others (Kennedy & Prock, 2018; Overstreet & Quinn, 2013; Williams & Mickelson, 2008). Racial-ethnic minority survivors are especially at risk for discrimination due to their racial-ethnic heritage (Stockman et al., 2015). This prejudice can be a large barrier that pushes survivors away from seeking formal support services (Rodríguez et al., 2009). Furthermore, racial-ethnic minority survivors who have dealt with prejudice and stigmatization in the past might have a heightened sense of anticipated stigma. One example of anticipated fear is the fear that a survivor might not be able to communicate with service care providers who do not understand their language, which can greatly affect a survivor's desire to seek formal help (Alegría et al., 2002; Rodríguez et al., 2009). This type of anticipated cultural and community fear can make it incredibly difficult for survivors looking for help and resources.

Shame as a Barrier to Help-Seeking

Emotion psychologists continue to research and make distinctions between basic and higher-level emotions felt by humans. According to prominent emotion researchers, there are six basic emotions that are widely used: happiness, sadness, fear, anger, surprise, and disgust (Ekman et al., 1972). There is consistent evidence to link these emotions with universal facial expressions, showing that basic emotions can be felt by all humans (Ekman, 1992). Further research has said that there are eight primary emotions that can be paired to show opposites: joy, sadness, anger, fear, acceptance, disgust, expectancy, and surprise (Plutchik, 1984). These basic, or primary, emotions affect how humans handle fundamental life tasks (Ekman, 1992). These six emotions have also been linked not only to humans, but to other animals as well, which proves how primary emotions have certain evolutionary qualities to them (Ortony & Turner, 1990). Emotions like shame, pride, and others outside of the basic emotions category are described as higher-level, secondary emotions which are conceptualized as complex emotions that follow a primary emotion (Kemper, 1987). For the purpose of this study, we will examine the higher-level emotion of shame and how this emotions affects help-seeking decisions among survivors from different racial-ethnic heritages.

Prior literature highlights many internal and external barriers to help-seeking. One of the most pervasive and all-encompassing barriers to help-seeking is the emotion of shame which can be felt at both the interpersonal level and intrapersonal level. Shame is described as a negative self-evaluation that includes feeling "bad," or "immoral" (Sheikh, 2014, p. 388). Literature around shame describes shame as an intense loss of either internal feelings about oneself or an external loss of status or reputation from culture or society (Blum, 2008; Gilbert, 1997; Murray et al., 2018; J. P. Wilson et al., 2006). Shame is closely related to interpersonal stigma and is a noteworthy outcome for people who have experienced IPV (Beck et al., 2015; Murray et al., 2018). Thus, feelings of shame can result from the internalization of societal messages about stigma and is closely related to stigma. This internalization can result from both overt and subliminal cues about the stigmatized experience such as societal beliefs that survivors invite their abuse (Overstreet & Quinn, 2013). Survivors' awareness of these beliefs can result in shame and the fear that no one will believe them and their experience (Simmons et al., 2011). Whether survivors are contemplating disclosure to formal service providers such as the police, medical or social service providers, or informal support providers such as friends and family, feelings of shame often prevent survivors of IPV from reaching out for help (Dunlop et al., 2005; Kennedy & Prock, 2018; Overstreet & Quinn, 2013). These negative beliefs about IPV can increase shame and stigma while also affecting help-seeking within a survivor's community (Thaggard & Montayre, 2019). For example, shame has been related to negative cultural stigma about IPV and help-seeking, making it difficult for IPV survivors to leave their abusive partner (Crandall et al., 2005; Rizo & Macy, 2011).

As a complex and higher-level emotion, shame can be felt at the societal and personal arenas (Kennedy & Prock, 2018). At the personal level, shame has been defined as, "an intensely painful feeling or experience of believing we are flawed and therefore unworthy of acceptance and belonging" (Brown, 2006, p. 45). Shame has also been PTSD symptoms which can follow a survivor for their whole life and affect their daily routines and relationships (Beck et al., 2011; Beck et al., 2015; Dodson & Beck, 2017; D. A. Lee et al., 2001). Not only is PTSD associated with shame, mental health problems like anxiety and depression have also been linked to the experience of shame among survivors of violence (Shorey et al., 2011). These long-term problems associated with shame can negatively affect a survivor if they do not seek-help for their trauma.

Societal shame focuses on the loss of attractive qualities of a person (Gilbert 1997; Velleman, 2001). Messages from society reinforce the idea that IPV is a normal and common occurrence, and this misinformation around IPV brings shame upon the victim instead of the person who inflicted the violence (McCleary-Sills et al., 2016). Because of these beliefs, survivors of IPV could face immense difficulties when trying to get out of their abusive situation. Shame also often leads survivors to isolate themselves which can, in turn, facilitate ongoing victimization (Bauer et al., 2000). The burden of shame is then placed onto the person who experienced violence instead of the perpetrator who caused the violence (Kam & Bond, 2009;

Koss, 2000; Mills, 2008) however, little is known about the intersection of shame with a person's culture and race-ethnicity while a survivor navigates the help-seeking process.

Racial-Ethnic Differences in Help-Seeking and Shame

Ethnicity plays a major role in whether a survivor of IPV seeks help from an external person due to historically discriminatory practices and barriers put in place for racial-ethnic minority survivors. Ongoing historical discrimination and maltreatment from people in positions of power force many racial-ethnic minority survivors to forgo formal services, like the police, for fear of unfair treatment due to their race or ethnicity (Decker et al., 2019; Wolf et al., 2003), and survivors often do not report their abusers to the police (Kasturirangan et al., 2004). A person's race or ethnic background can thus influence the desirability of help-seeking and from whom to seek help (Flicker et al., 2011; Liang et al., 2005; Lipsky et al., 2006). Most female survivors of IPV prefer to seek social support from trusted others like friends or family before seeking formal services (Flicker et al., 2011; Mahapatro & Gupta, 2014). Racial-ethnic minority women are particularly more likely to disclose to informal support providers, like friends, than formal support providers, such as the police (Bent-Goodley, 2007; Ingram, 2007; Stockman et al., 2015). A person's racial-ethnicity identity not only affects their help-seeking desires but can also affect how a person emotionally appraises IPV.

Although shame has been conceptualized as a universal and distinct human emotion (Tangney et al., 2005; Tracy & Matsumoto, 2008), the way that shame is felt and experienced may differ across cultures. Research suggests that individuals who place a high value on female submissiveness and family may believe that it is shameful to get a divorce or leave an abuser (Bauer et al., 2000; Satyen et al., 2019). There is also a strong desire to keep families intact, and family is incorporated into most decisions, leading some survivors of IPV to feel shame and stay with their abuser instead of seeking help (Crandall et al., 2005). Given the potentially important role of racial-ethnic heritage in help-seeking desires, the following section will explore the racial-ethnic differences influences on help-seeking and the experience of shame for IPV survivors.

Mexican and Latinx Racial-Ethnic Heritage IPV Survivors

For survivors belonging to Mexican and Latinx racial-ethnic identities, barriers to helpseeking involve distrust of the legal system, gendered norms, the prioritization of family, and cultural norms that stigmatize IPV. According to previous literature, Mexican/Latinx racialethnic heritage survivors tend to seek help from informal services like family instead of formal services like law enforcement or shelters (de Mendoza, 2001; Ingram, 2007; Rizo & Macy, 2011; Sabina et al., 2012). Research in this area has found that Latina female survivors will use informal services (76.6%) more often than formal services (32.5%; Sabina et al., 2012). The majority of Latino/x survivors utilize family or community instead of formal help-seeking opportunities because it follows cultural norms about keeping problems within the family (Bauer et al., 2000; de Mendoza, 2001). Along the same lines, the concept of not wanting to cause distress or conflict to others, known as

"simpatia," greatly affects help-seeking desires (Ahrens et

al., 2010; Triandis et al., 1984).

There is also a deep distrust of legal systems for some Mexican/Latinx racial-

ethnic survivors of IPV, making it even more difficult to seek help from formal

services like the police (Messing et al., 2015; Messing et al., 2017; Reina et al.,

2014). The phrase "La ropa sucia se lava en su casa," (i.e., dirty laundry should be

washed at home) is a common Latinx saying that means that people should keep

their problems within the household and that nonfamily members should not be

involved with family issues (Edelson et al., 2007; Flicker et al., 2011, Reina et al.,

2014). Another term, "familismo," encompasses the culture and family structure of

Mexican/Latinx culture that prioritizes family unity and well-being over individual

well-being (Bauer et al., 2000; Fuchsel et al., 2012; Mookerjee et al., 2015).

Through subliminal and explicit cultural norms, Mexican survivors of IPV are thus

faced with many barriers to help-seeking.

Some people who are of Mexican and Latinx heritage often organize their

self-perception and social status around honor and shame (Fontes, 2007), both of

which can be experienced at the individual or family level (Mookerjee et al., 2015;

Voth Schrag et al., 2021). When Mexican/Latinx survivors seek help for IPV, they

not only jeopardize their personal sense of honor and shame, but they also

jeopardize their family's honor (Dietrich & Schuett, 2013). If a survivor does seek

help, they often experience blame for the abuse they have endured, which leads to

shame since, according to society, the survivor somehow deserved the abuse (Voth

Schrag et al., 2021). In one study, shame was discussed by Hispanic survivors but not by nonHispanic survivors, and Hispanic survivors stated that shame led to social isolation which further pushed these survivors away from seeking help (Mookerjee et al., 2015). These cultural taboos and stigmatization of IPV pushes survivors of Mexican/Latinx heritage further away from seeking help (Denham et al., 2007), and the isolating experience of shame for Mexican/Latinx survivors can greatly alter a survivor's decision to seek help or not.

Asian American Racial-Ethnic Heritage IPV Survivors

Shame is also often imposed upon Asian American communities. Historically, Asian Americans are often compared to other racial-ethnic groups as a stereotyped model minority, and this pressure to be perfect often comes with deleterious effects to a person's mental and physical health (Shih et al., 2019). The societal pressure to fit into the model minority stereotype has been shown to place Asian Americans in a world where they feel like a foreigner in their own country, truly not feeling like they are American or Asian (P. Y. Kim & Lee, 2014; Y. S. Lee & Hadeed, 2009). These expectations to conform to Westernized culture while also upholding expectations within a person's family can leave Asian Americans feeling like an imposter and can lead to psychological distress or the feeling of shame (Cokley et al., 2013; Wei et al., 2020).

Westernized views conceptualize shame as an individual experience whereas collectivistic ideals and family structures, that some Asian Americans associate with, view the feeling shame as something that is felt in relationship with others (Y.

Wong & Tsai, 2007). Some Asian Americans have reported that in order to live up to stereotypes placed upon them and to not bring shame onto their family, there is a large pressure to succeed and fit into a world that was made for them instead of a world they created for themselves (Fouad et al., 2008); however, this notion that Asian Americans experience high levels of shame is one that tends to be inferred by Western scholars rather than something that has emerged from within the Asian community itself (Y. Wong & Tsai, 2007). It is true that the feeling of shame has been linked to Asian American culture and this feeling of shame has been tied to many different Asian racial-ethnic heritages in tandem with the concept of losing face (Ho et al., 2004; Venkateswaran, 2018). Indeed, the concept of shame and saving or losing face has been given specific verbiage and language in Chinese, Japanese, Vietnamese, Korean, and other racial-ethnic heritages (Bedford, 2004; Bui, 2003; Ho et al., 2004; Yang & Rosenblatt, 2001); however, literature often fails differentiate between Asian Americans from different ethnic backgrounds (Holland & Palaniappan, 2012; Yom & Lor, 2021). This current study challenges this generalized categorization by examining differences among Vietnamese and Korean racial-ethnic heritage survivors of IPV, in particular.

Korean racial-ethnic heritage IPV survivors. Some research suggests that up to 60% of Korean immigrant women in America experience some form of IPV in their lifetime, but only 17% sought help from a professional and 3% utilized police (Song, 1986). Even with a high lifetime prevalence, help-seeking among Korean survivors is quite low, and IPV is often underreported. Korean survivors of IPV face a variety of barriers to help-seeking that include cultural norms, language barriers, and gendered norms. Overall, Korean IPV survivors do not have high disclosure rates to either informal or formal networks (J. Y. Kim & Lee, 2011). One study indicated that only 15% of Korean IPV survivors sought help from informal support providers while 52% sought help from formal support providers like medical care (J. Y. Kim & Lee, 2011). For Korean survivors, specific cultural norms and gendered expectations may suppress disclosures. Cultural beliefs that justify abuse due to a woman's disobedience and actions (Yoshioka et al., 2001) and emphasize women's duty to keep abusive problems within the family can also make it difficult to seek help (Liles et al., 2012; W. S. Shim & NelsonBecker, 2009; Song 1986). Language can also be a barrier for Korean IPV survivors who often have difficulty locating Korean-language IPV services, causing survivors to isolate themselves instead of seeking help (J. Y. Kim & Sung, 2000; Kim-Goh & Baello, 2008). Cultural beliefs and family expectations can also result in women not being supported when trying to leave their partner (Choi et al., 2019), leading many Korean survivors to protect themselves from shame by not exposing themselves to potential negative reactions in the first place.

For some IPV survivors of Korean descent, shame is tied to not only individual shame, but familial shame as well (Yang & Rosenblatt, 2001). Individual shame and pressure can come from a desire to keep issues private and internal (Choi, 2015). This pressure can conflict with survivors' need to protect themselves through seeking external help and the survivors' desire to protect the family from greater cultural shame (Choi et al., 2019; Green et al., 2023). Patriarchal societies, like that of some Korean-heritage survivors, associate shame with disclosure of personal matters to those outside of the immediate family. Pressures from society can shame a survivor into silence instead of supporting a survivor to seek help (Park et al., 2021; Sylaska & Edwards, 2014). Other factors like obedience, honor, and respect tied to cultural values can greatly affect a survivor's desire to seek help. Cultural concepts like obedience and respect to one's family places the needs of the family above an individual's needs, which can deter survivors from looking externally for help after experiencing violence (W. S. Shim & NelsonBecker, 2009). The interlocking concepts of dishonor and shame can be a large barrier for survivors seeking help from outside of their specific community (Green et al., 2023). All of these experiences and beliefs around shame can affect a Korean heritage IPV survivor's decision to seek help because the situation no longer only involves just themselves as individuals, it involves their family name as well.

Vietnamese racial-ethnic heritage IPV survivors. Vietnamese IPV survivors also face barriers to help-seeking. Statistics show that Asian Americans are less likely to seek help for problems, including physical abuse and mental health problems stemming from abuse (Leung & Cheung, 2008). Vietnamese survivors are least likely out of other Asian populations to seek help from mental health professionals and service agencies like a women's shelter (Appel et al., 2011). For Vietnamese survivors of IPV, less than one third of survivors sought any help from formal entities like social services or counseling to discuss help-seeking options (Morash et al.,

2008), while informal options like friends and family more often used by Vietnamese survivors (Bui, 2003; Leung & Cheung, 2008; Kim-Mozeleski et al.,

2018). Culture greatly effects helpseeking decisions and affects most aspects of people's lives. Vietnamese survivors who supported traditional, collectivistic cultures were significantly more likely to be abused by their partner and significantly less likely to seek help for the abuse in order to protect others by avoiding disclosure (Bui & Morash, 2007; Y. S. Lee & Hadeed, 2009). Vietnamese participants in one study found that 60% supported ideals that men should run the home, and around one fourth of Vietnamese participants in the same study said that a man should be able to have sex with his wife whenever he desires (Yoshioka et al., 2001). These patriarchal and gendered roles within the family structure prohibit women from seeking help, and there is a deeply held belief that problems should be dealt within the family, in turn isolating the survivor (Cho, 2012; Do et al., 2013; Shiu-Thornton et al., 2005). One study found that 54.2% of respondents supported the idea that a husband should be allowed to discipline their wife (Chang et al., 2009). In these ways,

Vietnamese traditional and collectivistic familial roles play a large role in a survivor's decision to seek help for their experience with IPV.

    Furthermore, much of Vietnamese heritage, family, and community revolves around respect and honor. Expressions of shame can be best described as "losing face," which is the experience a person goes through when they have lost respect from the community at large (Do et al., 2013; Zane & Yeh, 2002). This shameful experience of "face" or the need to "face save" can be seen as an internal and external feeling (Do et al., 2013 p. 150). Internally, survivors of

IPV could be pushed into silence due to the pressure of not wanting to "lose face" and shame the people that the survivor loves and cares about through disclosure (Pham, 2014). Externally, there is shame and dishonor when a person experiences "losing face" and is ostracized from the community at large (Ahrens et al., 2021; Bui, 2003). The experience of shame can thus prevent survivors from seeking help through professional means (i.e., the police) or through informal routes (i.e., friends) due to lack of perceived support from their community (Bui, 2003). As a result of such concerns, Asian survivors of IPV often feel that problems within the family should stay within the family (Bauer et al., 2000; Berg & Jaya, 1993). Feelings around "losing face," internal, and external pressures are all experiences Vietnamese IPV survivors can experience involving shame and help-seeking.

European (White) Racial-Ethnic Heritage IPV Survivors

Although survivors of European (White) heritage are more likely to utilize resources than survivors of color, White women are still unlikely to seek any help at all, be that from formal or informal resources (Ingram, 2007). When it comes to mental health help-seeking, White women are more likely to seek services that address their mental health needs than racial-ethnic minority survivors (Cheng & Lo, 2015; Flicker et al., 2011). This could largely be due to the fact that European (White) women have historically had more access to services (Kasturirangan et al., 2004), but it could also be that European (White) women have also been studied more. Indeed, more recent research, has found that racial-ethnic identity did not affect overall help-seeking tendencies for violence survivors (Cho et al., 2020; Flicker et al., 2011), and one study found that

White women were less likely to report IPV to the police than Black and Hispanic survivors of IPV (Lipsky et al., 2009). These conflicting findings point to the need for more research comparing help-seeking among survivors from different racial-ethnic backgrounds.

Compared to women of color, European (White) IPV survivors tend to experience shame in a much more individualistic and personal way that is often intertwined with personal feelings of guilt (Fessler, 2004; Warren, 2010). European heritage (White) survivors also report feeling self-blame and anticipatory stigma which keeps them from seeking help (Heath et al., 2011; Voth Schrag et al., 2021). For some European heritage (White) survivors, religion can also increase feelings of shame. Some religions, like Catholicism and the Church of Jesus Christ of Latter-day Saints, do not support divorce and promote shame amongst religious individuals who think about leaving or reporting an abusive relationship (Gezinski et al., 2019; Ware et al., 2004). As a result, certain religions can act as a shameful barrier to a survivor leaving an abusive situation, serving as a powerful tool that shames survivors into silence (Ware et al., 2004); however, other research suggests that European (White) survivors report feeling less shame than racial-ethnic minority survivors (Sylaska & Edwards, 2014), a finding that needs further empirical exploration due to the sparse research comparing shame across diverse racial-ethnic IPV survivors. Altogether past research suggests that there could be differences between both shame and help-seeking tendencies among different racial-ethnic populations, little is known about the role of racialethnic heritage as a moderating factor between shame and help-seeking, and the current study aims to address this deficit in the literature.

Current Study

Most IPV research has been conducted on populations that are western, educated, industrialized, rich, and democratic (W.E.I.R.D., Henrich et al., 2010). Yet these people are not representative of the larger population, this specific population is very small, and researchers should take their sample representation into consideration when generalizing about the human experience. External validity can come into question if researchers do not use racially-ethnically diverse samples (Henrich et al., 2010). This is particularly true of research on IPV. Most IPV studies lack representation of racially and ethnically diverse female-identified survivors of IPV, and there is a large deficit in understanding and information on how to assist these women as they seek-help and emotionally appraise their experience with IPV. The current study is thus part of the call to action for diversifying research in the IPV field (Cuevas & Cudmore, 2017; Y. S. Lee & Hadeed, 2009; Stockman et al., 2015).

Specifically, the current study will examine the relationship between shame, racial-ethnic heritage, and help-seeking behaviors among Mexican, Korean, Vietnamese, and European (White) survivors of intimate partner violence. It is hypothesized that:

1. Mexican, Korean, and Vietnamese racial-ethnic heritage IPV survivors will have higher levels of shame than European (White) heritage survivors.

2. Higher levels of shame will lead to lower help-seeking.

3. The relationship between shame and help-seeking will vary depending on racial-ethnic heritage. Specifically, the relationship between shame and help-seeking will be stronger among IPV survivors of Mexican, Korean, and Vietnamese descent than among IPV survivors of European (White) descent.

CHAPTER 2

METHOD

Procedures

The data from this study was part of a larger study that investigated how culture influenced IPV survivors' experiences of violence (Mechanic & Ahrens, 2019). Data was collected throughout the year of 2017. The study design for the larger study involved purposive sampling of IPV survivors of Mexican, Korean, Vietnamese, and European racial-ethnic descent. Recruitment for both qualitative interviews and online surveys occurred simultaneously. Initial recruitment involved pamphlets, local newspaper advertisements, and in-person presentations at social service agencies, cultural centers, and health fairs in Los Angeles County and Orange County. Materials were also distributed to local businesses frequented by women such as nail salons, gyms, and recreation facilities. In all, over 1,500 establishments were utilized to recruit participants for this study. This adaptive sampling method provided researchers with the ability to purposefully sample from specific locations where target populations are abundant for researchers in this study (R. Campbell et al., 2004; S. K. Thompson, 1997). We utilized this method to target places where female Mexican, Korean, Vietnamese, and European (White) individuals lived, worked, and frequented.

Recruitment efforts invited adult women from one of four target racial-ethnic heritage identities to participate in an online survey. To qualify for this study, the female-identified participant must have experienced IPV within the past 5 years, identified as female, were over the age of 18, and were part of the four-target racial-ethnic heritage groups. Recruitment materials were available in each of the four

target group languages which were Spanish, Korean,

Vietnamese, and English. All recruitment and study materials were translated and

back translated into from English into the target languages. Specialists in each

language then reviewed all translated materials to check for and correct any remaining

translation errors.

Recruitment efforts occurred throughout Los Angeles and Orange County,

which covered 51 cities in total. Participants interested in completing a survey were

provided with a direct link to the Qualtrics survey. After choosing their preferred

language (Spanish, Korean, Vietnamese, and English), survey participants were

taken to an Informed Consent page where risks and benefits of participation were

fully explained. Surveys typically took around an hour to complete. Once finished,

participants received a $20 gift card for Amazon.com., a list of referrals, and safety

planning information.

Participants

Out of the 193 online survey participants, 32.1% were of Mexican racial-

ethnic heritage descent, 21.8% were of Korean heritage descent, 20.2% were of

Vietnamese heritage descent, and 25.9% were of European heritage (White)

descent. Table 1 discusses racial-ethnic differences in demographic characteristics

by showing the overall percentage of participants who identified with the statement,

and the subsequent columns shows the percentages of people within specific racial-

ethnic identities who also identified with that statement meaning that each column

compares within that same racial-ethnic identity. For example, less than half of the participants in this study were born in the United States of America, with IPV

survivors of Vietnamese and Korean racial-ethnic decent least likely to be born in

the United States of America (U.S.A.) compared to other Vietnamese and Korean

IPV survivors in this study. The majority of participants in this study stated that

their preferred languages were English, then Spanish, Korean, and Vietnamese,

with over half of Mexican and Vietnamese racial-ethnic identity participant

utilizing English for this study. Similarly, surveys were mostly conducted in

English, then Spanish, Korean, and with the smallest amount of surveys being

conducted in Vietnamese. At home, within participants from European (White)

racial-ethnic identities 96% spoke English at home and within Mexican racial-

ethnic heritage participants over half preferred to speak English at home and the

other half preferred Spanish as can be seen in Table 1.

These participants were on average 35.02 years old (SD = 11.80, range = 18-71).

Survivors varied in their level of education with ¼ having a high school degree or

less. Specifically, when Mexican IPV survivors were compared to Mexican IPV

survivors in this study, almost half of these Mexican racial-ethnic heritage IPV

survivors had a high school education or less in this sample. Household incomes

also varied with 21.8% of participants receiving less than $20,000 per year and

6.7% of participants having a household income of over $100,000 per year. Slightly

under half of the Mexican racial-ethnic heritage survivors in this study, when

compared to other Mexican participants in this study, had a household income of

$38,000 or less (Table 1). Over half (56.6%) of participants were no longer

romantically involved with their abuser; however, Vietnamese IPV survivors in this study when compared to other Vietnamese IPV survivors in this study showed that 62.2% were still in a relationship with their abuser (Table 1). Out of these participants, almost all had told at least one person (93.5%) about their experience of abuse. All but one Vietnamese IPV survivor (99.5%) had experienced at least one form of psychological abuse, most survivors (80.1%) experienced at least one form of physical abuse with Korean IPV survivors (68.3%) experiencing the least amount of physical abuse compared to all Korean survivors in this study, and many experienced sexual abuse (72.1%) with Korean IPV survivors (80.5%) experiencing the most sexual abuse within all of this study's Korean IPV sample.

TABLE 1. Racial-Ethnic Heritage Differences in Demographic Characteristics

Variable	Overall	Mexican	Korean	Vietnamese	European (White)	X_2
	Percent	Percent	Percent	Percent	Percent	
Relationship						
Still with Abuser	43.4	41[a]	45[ab]	62.2[b]	30.6[1]	.03*
English Spoken Most Often at Home	51.8	54.8[a]	16.7[b]	28.2[b]	96[c]	<.001*
Born in the U.S.A.	47.7	51.6[a]	7.1[b]	23.1[c]	96[d]	<.001*
Survey						

[1] Note: Statistical significance was measured at $p < .05$*. [b]Note: Means sharing a superscript were not significantly different from one another

Conducted in English	62.7	66.1[a]	23.8[b]	51.3[a]	100[c]	<.001*
High School Education or Less	24.4	43.5[a]	4.8[b]	35.9[a]	8[b]	<.001*
Household Income of 38k or Less	36.8	48.4[a]	23.4[b]	41[ab]	30[b]	.048*
35 Years Old or Younger	42	46.8[a]	52.4[a]	17.9[b]	46[a]	.007*
Psychological Abuse Any	99.5	100	100	97.4	100	.27
Physical Abuse Any	80.1	87.1[a]	68.3[b]	84.6[ab]	77.6[ab]	.10
Sexual Abuse Any	72.8	66.1	80.5	69.2	77.6	.33

Measures

Online surveys were offered in Spanish, Korean, Vietnamese, and English. For the current study, only the data pertaining to shame and help-seeking were used.

Shame

Perceptions of shame were assessed using DePrince et al.'s (2010) Trauma Appraisal Questionnaire (TAQ). This is a 54-item scale that measures how a person appraises their emotions after a traumatic event. The six subscales in this questionnaire are: betrayal, self-blame, fear, alienation, anger, and shame (DePrince et al., 2010). For this study we will focus on one of these subscales: shame

(Appendix A). Participants were asked to answer questions on a scale from 1 (strongly disagree) to 5 (strongly agree) on questions like, "No shower could wash away how dirty I felt," or "I felt ashamed." These items were then averaged, with higher scores indicating a higher sense of shame. The reliability and validity of the TAQ have been assessed in previous research through three samples: two were undergraduate populations and one community population of survivors of IPV. A Cronbach's alpha (α = .90) for the TAQ was found across these three samples, indicating strong internal reliability for this questionnaire (DePrince et al., 2010). In the current study Cronbach's alpha for the TAQ shame subscale was high (α = .91), indicating a high level of internal consistency for this subscale with our specific research sample.

Help-Seeking

Help-seeking was assessed through questions focused on who the survivor told about their IPV situation. In order to assess help-seeking, a series of dichotomous questions were developed for this study: "Were the police called?," "Have you told clergy?," "Have you told doctors?," "Have you told counselors?," "Have you told advocates?," "Have you told members of your birth family?," "Have you told friends?," "Have you told members not in your family?," and "Have you told acquaintances?" (Appendix B). Participants answered yes or no to these questions, yielding separate variables that indicated whether or not survivors had disclosed to each type of support provider. These variables were then combined into three calculated variables: whether survivors had disclosed to any informal support providers (friends, family, acquaintances), whether survivors had disclosed to any

formal support providers (police, doctors, clergy, counselors, advocates), and

whether survivors had disclosed to anyone at all (Appendix B). Each calculated

item was scored as 1 (sought help) or 0 (did not seek help).

CHAPTER 3

RESULTS

Preliminary Results

Descriptive Statistics

Frequencies and chi-square analyses were run on the main variables of this study which were the TAQ shame subscale items and help-seeking options. Overall, there was a moderate endorsement of shame with an average scale score of 2.57 out of a scale of 1 to 5. Table 2 shows that over sixty percent of IPV survivor participants in this study agreed or strongly agreed with the statements, "I felt humiliated," "I felt ashamed," and "I felt embarrassed." Table 3 represents racial-ethnic heritage differences on the TAQ shame subscale items.

TABLE 2. Frequency Table of the TAQ Shame Subscale Items

Variable	Characteristic	Frequency ($n = 193$)	Percent
TAQ: I lost my sense of womanhood.	Strongly Agree	37	19.2
	Agree	51	26.4
	Disagree	51	26.4
	Strongly Disagree	46	23.8
	Missing	8	4.2
TAQ: I felt humiliated.	Strongly Agree	67	34.7
	Agree	65	33.7
	Disagree	23	11.9

	Strongly Disagree	34	17.6
	Missing	8	4.2
TAQ: I felt ashamed.	Strongly Agree	59	30.6
	Agree	65	33.7

TABLE 2. Continued

	Disagree	27	14
	Strongly Disagree	34	17.6
	Missing	8	4.2
TAQ: I felt disgust.	Strongly Agree	53	27.5
	Agree	64	33.2
	Disagree	31	16.1
	Strongly Disagree	38	19.7
	Missing	7	3.7
TAQ: I felt embarrassed.	Strongly Agree	61	31.6
	Agree	67	34.7
	Disagree	27	14
	Strongly Disagree	31	16.1
	Missing	7	3.7
TAQ: It's as if my insides were dirty.	Strongly Agree	22	11.4
	Agree	35	18.1
	Disagree	61	31.6
	Strongly Disagree	64	33.2
	Missing	11	5.7
TAQ: No shower could wash away how dirty I felt.	Strongly Agree	24	12.4

Agree	40	20.7
Disagree	50	25.9
Strongly Disagree	67	34.7

TABLE

3. Racial-Ethnic Heritage Differences for Individual TAQ Shame Subscale Items

Variable	Overall	Mexican		Korean		Vietnamese		European (White)		F
	M	M	SD	M	SD	M	SD	M	SD	
"I felt embarrassed."	3.12	2.80bc	1.23	2.78c	1.12	2.57bc	1.01	3.23a	0.84	2.90*
"I felt disgust."	3.30	2.44b	1.15	2.78	1.05	2.57	1.04	3.05a	1.02	2.86*
"I felt ashamed."	2.06	2.75	1.09	2.75	1.11	2.49	1.04	3.05	1.05	1.79
"I felt humiliated."	3.01	2.98a	1.04	2.92ab	1.05	2.51b	1.07	3.19a	1.01	2.78*
"It's as if my insides were dirty."	0.36	2.15	1.01	2.14	0.99	1.94	0.99	2.12	1.07	0.35
"I lost my sense of womanhood."	1.46	2.63	1.11	2.47	1.11	2.26	1.04	2.28	1.03	1.26
"No shower could wash away how dirty I felt."	0.49	2.12	1.07	2.22	1.07	1.94	0.97	2.14	1.10	0.44

[a]Note: Statistical significance was measured at $p < .05$*. [b]Note: Means sharing a superscript were not significantly different from one another

The next step was to examine who these participants disclosed to and the racial-ethnic differences in who was disclosed to most frequently. The descriptive analyses suggested that participants disclosed their experience with trauma at fairly

TABLE

high rates (93.6%). Overall, the highest number of participants disclosed to informal support providers like friends as opposed to formal service providers like the police (Table 4). Participants in this study disclosed in moderately high rates to formal, informal, and a combination of formal and informal service providers.

4. Frequency Table of Help-Seeking Options

Variable	Characteristic	Frequency (n = 193)	Percent
Disclosure – Any	Yes	175	90.7
	No	12	6.2
	Missing	6	3.1
Formal Disclosure – Any	Yes	137	71.0
	No	49	25.4
	Missing	7	3.6
Informal Disclosure – Any	Yes	164	85.0
	No	21	10.9
	Missing	8	4.1

Racial-ethnic heritage differences in help-seeking desires for formal, informal, or a combination of service care providers were then analyzed. While there were no significant racialethnic differences in overall disclosure or disclosure to informal support sources, there were racial-ethnic differences in rates of disclosure to formal support providers. Specifically, Vietnamese participants sought help from formal support providers at significantly lower rates than any other

racial-ethnic heritage identity, and these differences were reflected in each specific

type of formal support provider, as well (Table 5). Of note, nearly half of all Korean

racial-ethnic heritage survivors had disclosed to clergy or other religious personnel

and advocates, and both Korean and Vietnamese survivors were significantly less

likely to have disclosed to family.

5. Racial-Ethnic Heritage Differences for Any, Formal, and Informal Help-Seeking

Variable	Overall	Mexican	Korean	Vietnamese	European (White)	X_2
	Percent	Percent	Percent	Percent	Percent	

	Total					p
Disclosure: Formal Any	74.7	88.1[a]	67.5[b]	36.8[c]	89.8[a]	<.001*
Formal: Police	34.1	44.6[a]	29.7	7.9[b]	43.5[a]	<.001*
Formal: Clergy or Other Religious	30.9	31.0[a]	44.7[a]	13.2[b]	34[a]	<.001*
Formal: Doctors or Other Medical	22.7	25.0[ab]	5.6[c]	16.7[bc]	37.5[a]	.005*
Formal: Counselors or Other Mental Health	50.6	62.1[a]	47.4[a]	22.2[b]	60.4[a]	<.001*
Formal: Advocates or Other Community	35.6	39.3[a]	44.7[a]	10.5[b]	43.8[a]	.004*
Disclosure: Informal Any	88.6	88.1	95.0	84.2	87.5	.49
Informal: Your Birth Family	59.2	74.1[a]	52.5[b]	42.1[b]	60.4[ab]	.013*
Informal: Partner's Family	32.6	45.6[a]	28.9[ab]	18.4[b]	31.3[ab]	.043*
Informal: Friends	70.0	64.3	79.5	68.4	70.2	.46
Informal:	40.9	45.6	43.6	37.8	35.4	.71

TABLE

TABLE

Acquaintances [a]Note: Statistical significance was measured at $p <$ .05*. [b]Note: Means sharing a superscript were not significantly different from one another

Finally, correlations between demographic variables and average shame ratings were explored. Appendix C showed that relationship status, if a person was born in the U.S.A., if a person spoke English predominately at home, any physical abuse, and any sexual abuse were all significantly and positively correlated with average TAQ shame scores for participants in the current study. Current romantic involvement was the only demographic item that was negatively correlated with the average shame rating on the TAQ shame subscale, as average shame scores increased, participants were less likely to still be romantically involved with their abusive partner.

Power Analyses

A post hoc power analysis was conducted using G*Power version 3.1.9.6 (Faul et al.,

2007) to determine if the current sample size provides adequate for our proposed analyses for an

ANOVA. The obtained sample size of $n = 193$ was adequate to test this study's one-way

ANOVA for a medium effect with 83% power.

Additionally, a post hoc power analysis was conducted using G*Power version 3.1.9.6

(Faul et al., 2007) to determine if the current sample size ($n = 193$) could

show a small effect at 80% power utilizing data from Mechanic and

Ahrens, 2019. Post hoc results indicated that for logistic regression the

obtained sample size of $n = 193$ is adequate to test this study's hypobook

for a small effect with 92% power.

Racial-Ethnic Differences in Shame

Racial-Ethnic Differences in Average Levels of Shame

A one-way between subjects ANOVA was conducted to compare the effect of ethnic heritage on the average score of shame for Mexican, Korean, Vietnamese, and European (White) racial-ethnic heritage survivors of intimate partner violence. Inconsistent with the hypobook, results from a one-way between subjects ANOVA did not indicate a significant difference in feelings of shame between survivors of Mexican heritage ($M = 2.56$, $SD = .87$), Korean heritage ($M = 2.62$, $SD = .88$), Vietnamese heritage ($M = 2.31$, $SD = .85$), and European (White) heritage ($M = 2.75$, $SD = .80$), $F(3,184) = 1.921$, $p > .128$, $\eta^2 = .030$. According to this analysis, only 3% of the variance in the average experience of shame can be explained by racial-ethnic heritage. This suggests that there is no evidence to suggest that different racial-ethnic minority survivors reported more or less average shame than one another (Figure 1).

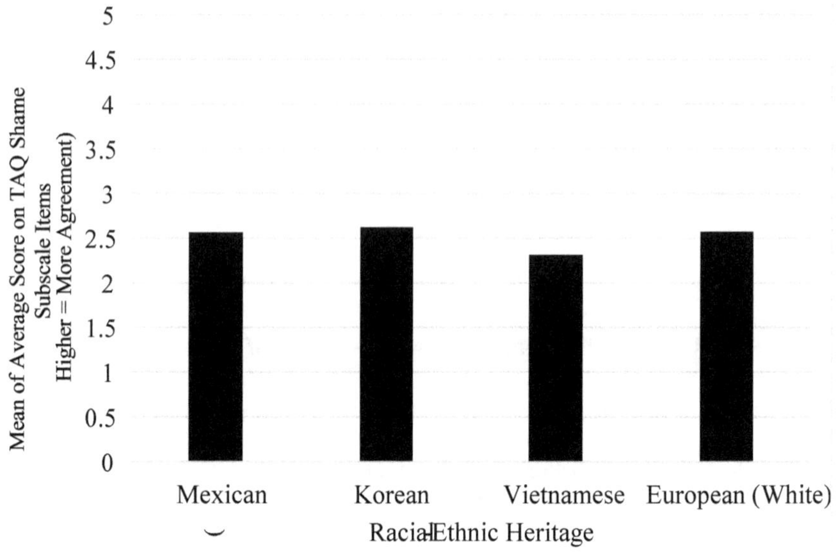

FIGURE 1. One-way ANOVA comparing average TAQ shame
subscale score with racialethnic heritage.

Racial-Ethnic Differences in Individual Shame Items

Although racial-ethnic differences in average levels of shame did not

emerge, it is still possible that there could be significant differences on

some of the seven specific items that make up the TAQ shame subscale. To

investigate if racial-ethnic heritage predicted higher levels of shame for

specific items on the shame subscale of the TAQ, a one-way multiple

analysis of variance (One-Way MANOVA) was conducted. A MANOVA

allows for the simultaneous analysis of multiple related dependent variables

(i.e., the 7 items in the TAQ shame subscale) to determine whether the

overall model is significant, which corrects for Type 1 error that can occur

when running multiple analyses. Results of the MANOVA suggested that there was a statistically significant difference between racial-ethnic heritage

identity within the overall model, Wilk's

(Λ) = 0.820, $F(21,469)$ = 1.60, $p < .045$; η^2= .064, observed power = .948.

The Wilk's Lambda (Λ) test, which serves as the omnibus test, proved

significant ($p < .045$) with an observed power of .948 which is higher than

the standard of .80 meaning that there was a 94.8% chance that the results

would have resulted in a significant finding. Based on these results, we can

reject the null hypobook and conclude that there was a significant

difference in at least one of the TAQ shame subscale items based on racial-

ethnic heritage identity.

To determine which items were driving these results, pair-wise

comparisons using univariate F-tests were examined. Table 3 results show

that there were significant racial-ethnic differences on the statements: "I

felt embarrassed," "I felt disgust," and "I felt humiliated." These findings

also mirror overall TAQ shame subscale frequency trends (Table 2).

Post-hoc pairwise comparisons revealed that European heritage
(White) survivors ($M =$

3.23, SD = .84) had significantly more embarrassment on the "I felt

embarrassed" statement compared to Mexican (M = 2.80 , SD = 1.13) and

Vietnamese (M = 2.57, SD = 1.01) racialethnic heritage survivors $F(3,169)$

= 2.90, $p < .037$, η^2 = .049, but there was no significant difference between

European (White; M = 3.23, SD = .84) and Korean (M = 2.78, SD = 1.12)

racial-ethnic heritage survivors on this statement (Table 3). Post-hoc

pairwise comparisons also revealed that for the statement "I felt disgust,"
European heritage (White; $M = 3.05$, $SD = 1.02$) survivors felt significantly
more disgust than their Mexican ($M = 2.44$, $SD = 1.15$) racial-ethnic
heritage survivor counterparts, but there were no significant differences
between European

(White) ($M = 3.05$, $SD = 1.02$), Vietnamese ($M = 2.57$, $SD = 1.04$), and
Korean ($M = 2.78$, $SD =$

1.05) racial-ethnic heritage survivor's feelings of disgust $F(3,169) = 2.86$, p
$< .039$, $\eta^2 = .048$

(Table 4). Finally, post-hoc pairwise comparisons for the statement "I felt
humiliated" showed that Mexican ($M = 2.98$, $SD = 1.09$) heritage survivors
felt significantly more humiliated than their Vietnamese ($M = 2.49$, $SD =$
1.04) heritage counterparts and that European (White; $M =$
3.19, $SD = 1.01$) heritage survivors felt significantly more humiliation than
their Vietnamese ($M = 2.51$, $SD = 1.07$) heritage survivor counterparts
$F(3,169) = 2.78$, $p < .043$, $\eta^2 = .047$ (Table 4), but there were no significant
differences between Korean ($M = 2.51$, $SD = 1.07$) racial-ethnic heritage
survivors and other racial-ethnic heritage survivors reported in this study.

No significant differences were found amongst the following TAQ
shame subscale statements: "It's as if my insides were dirty," "No shower
could wash away how dirty I felt," "I felt ashamed," and "I lost my sense of
womanhood."

Racial-Ethnic Differences in the Relationship between Shame and Help-Seeking

Disclosure to Any Support Provider

Hypotheses 2 and 3 were examined simultaneously with a moderated logistic regression using the PROCESS macro v4.0 for SPSS. Main effects for shame and racial-ethnic group were used to examine Hypobook 2 which postulated that higher levels of shame would lead to lower levels of help-seeking. For our first analysis, this hypobook was examined for overall helpseeking from any informal or formal service provider (i.e., did they disclose to anyone at all). To help isolate the impact of shame on help-seeking, the following covariates were also included in the model: if the survivor was still in a relationship with their abuser, the survivor's age at the time of the survey, the survivor's education level, the household income, whether the survey was conducted in English or not, if the survivor was born in the United States or outside of the United States, if the survivor spoke English at home or another language, if the participants had experienced psychological abuse, if the participant endured any physical abuse, and if the participants experienced any sexual abuse.

The results of this first moderated logistic regression indicated that there were no significant main effects or interactions, and none of the covariates were significantly related to help-seeking (Appendix D). We therefore chose to rerun the analyses without the covariates to free up some variance. Results of the moderated logistic regression without the covariates are reported in Table 6. These results indicated that there were no significant main effects for shame $\chi^2(1) = 1.5236$, $p = .138$ or racial-ethnic heritage on help-seeking for Korean ($\chi^2(1) = 1.38$, $p = .6368$), Vietnamese ($\chi^2(1) = 1.4403$, $p = .5638$), or Mexican ($\chi^2(1) = 4.3917$, $p = .1385$) survivors as compared to White survivors. These results contradict our hypobook that shame is related to overall help-seeking and also suggest that there are no racial-ethnic differences in help-seeking.

TABLE 6. Logistic Regression of Effects of Shame on Any Form of Help-Seeking with Moderation by Racial-Ethnic Group ($n = 184$)

Variable	Coefficient	SE	95% CI		p
			LL	UL	
Model Statistics: $\chi^2(7) = 7.287$, $p = .395$, McFadden $R^2 = .0821$					
Shame (X)	1.52	1.03	-.49	3.53	.14
Korean (W1)[a]	1.38	2.93	-4.35	7.12	.64
Vietnamese (W2)[a]	1.44	2.50	3.45	6.33	.56
Mexican (W3)[a]	4.39	2.96	-1.42	10.20	.14
Shame x Korean (XW1)[a]	-.70	1.18	-3.37	1.97	.61
Shame x Vietnamese (XW2)[a]	-1.13	1.18	-3.45	1.19	.34
Shame x Mexican (XW3)[a]	-1.91	1.25	-4.36	.54	.13

Shame x Ethnic Group (XW omnibus test): $\chi^2(3) = 2.903$, *p* > .407

Note. CI = Confidence Interval; LL = lower limit; UL = upper limit. ^{a}B = unstandardized beta coefficient [b]Reference group: European (White)

To test our third hypobook that the relationship between shame and help-seeking would be moderated by racial-ethnic heritage, we then examined the interaction terms in the moderated logistic regression. As can be seen in Table 6, results suggested that there were no significant main effects or interactions for overall disclosure. $\chi^2(7) = 7.287$, p = .395, McFadden $R^2 = .0821$, and the model predicted only 8.2% of the variance in help-seeking (Table 6). Additionally, our third hypobook that racial-ethnic heritage would moderate the association between shame and any type of disclosure was not significant $\chi^2(3) = 2.903$, *p* > .407, showing that the relationship between shame and overall disclosure was not moderated by racial-ethnic heritage (Figure 2). However, it is possible that shame might affect formal and informal help-seeking differently. To examine these potential differences, we reran our analyses separately for formal and informal help-seeking.

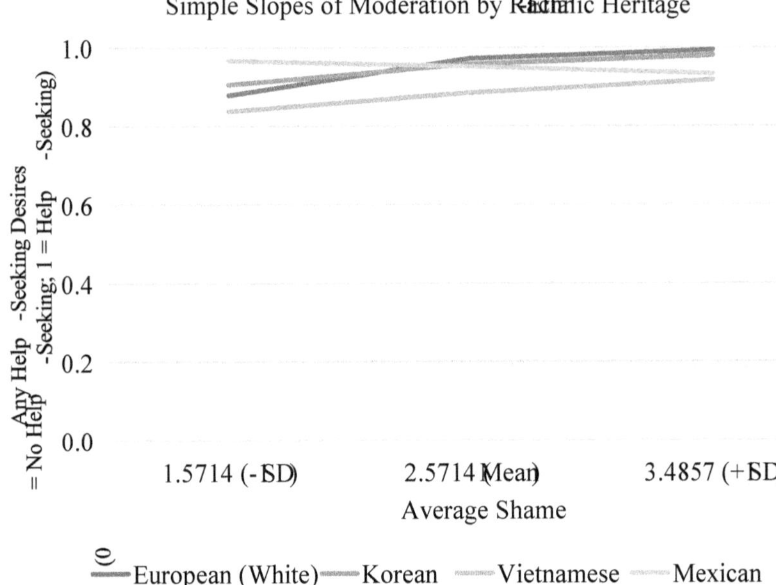

FIGURE 2. Simple slopes of moderation by racial-ethnic heritage for any disclosure.

Disclosure to Formal Support Providers

A moderated logistic regression model using the PROCESS macro v4.0 for SPSS was used to examine the relationship between shame and formal help-seeking among survivors of different racial-ethnic groups. The overall model was significant $\chi^2(7) = 49.967$, p < .001 McFadden $R^2 = .235$, predicting 24% of the variance in help-seeking with results shown in Table

6. Results suggested that there were no significant main effects for shame $\chi^2(1) = .6634$, $p = .27$ or racial-ethnic heritage on formal help-seeking for Korean ($\chi^2(1) = -3.027$, $p = .1007$),

Vietnamese ($\chi^2(1) = -.9704$, $p = .5930$), or Mexican ($\chi^2(1) = 2.3864$, $p = .2418$) survivors, compared to White survivors (Table 7).

TABLE 7. Logistic Regression of Effects of Shame on Formal Help-Seeking With Moderation by Racial-Ethnic Group ($n = 183$)

Variable	Coefficient	*SE*	95% CI		*p*
			LL	UL	
Model Statistics: $\chi^2(7) = 49.967$, $p < .001$ McFadden $R^2 = .235$					
Shame (X)	.66	.60	-.51	1.84	.27
Korean (W1)[a]	-3.30	2.01	-7.25	.64	.10
Vietnamese (W2)[a]	-.97	1.82	-4.53	2.59	.59
Mexican (W3)[a]	2.39	2.04	-1.61	6.38	.24
Shame x Korean (XW1)[a]	.77	.80	-.79	2.33	.33
Shame x Vietnamese (XW2)[a]	-.66	.72	-2.07	.76	.36
Shame x Mexican (XW3)[a]	-.97	.76	-2.46	.53	.21
Shame x Ethnic Group (XW omnibus test): $\chi^2(3) = 8.37$, $p < .039$					
Conditional Effects (Simple Slopes)					
European (White)	.66	.60	-.51	1.84	.27
Korean	1.44	.52	.41	2.46	.006*
Vietnamese	.01	.40	-.77	.79	.98
Mexican	-.30	.47	-1.23	.63	.52

Note. CI = Confidence Interval; LL = lower limit;
UL = upper limit. [a]B = unstandardized beta
coefficient [b]Reference group: European (White)

This contradicts our second hypobook that higher levels of shame

would lead to higher levels of help-seeking for formal outlets. However,

the interaction between shame and formal help-seeking was significant

$\chi^2(3) = 8.37$, $p < .039$, upholding our hypobook that the relationship

between shame and formal help-seeking is moderated by racial-ethnic

heritage (Table 7). Analysis of the simple slopes (see Figure 3) showed that

whereas shame was positively associated with help-seeking among women

of Korean descent ($B = 1.44$, $SE = .52$, $p = 0.006$), shame was not

significantly associated with help-seeking for Vietnamese ($B = .008$, $SE =$

.40, $p = .984$), Mexican ($B = -0.30$, $SE = .47$, $p = .523$), and European

(White) racial ethnic heritage survivors ($B = .66$, $SE = .60$, $p = .269$).

Further examination of conditional effects suggested that the relationship

between shame and help-seeking was stronger among Korean women than

European (White) women. As can be seen in Figure 3, the more shame

Korean survivors experienced, the more likely they were to have sought

help from formal outlets.

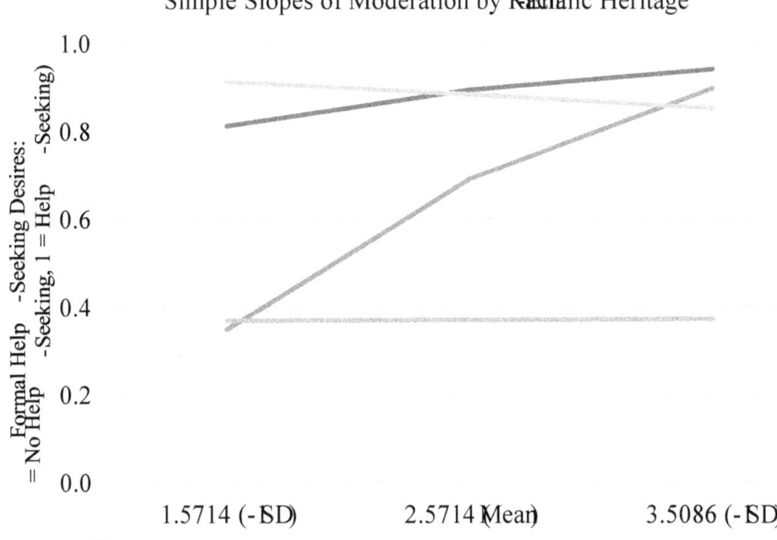

FIGURE 3. Simple slopes of moderation by racial-ethnic heritage for formal disclosure.

Disclosure to Informal Support Providers

To determine whether this effect is different for disclosure to informal support providers, a moderated logistic regression model using the PROCESS macro v4.0 for SPSS was used to examine the relationship between shame and informal help-seeking among survivors of different racial-ethnic groups. The overall model was not significant $\chi^2(7) = 4.30$, $p > .7447$ McFadden $R^2 = .0341$, predicting only 3.41% of the variance in help-seeking (Table 7). Results indicated that there were no significant main effects for shame $\chi^2(1) = .2736$, $p = .6485$ or racial-ethnic heritage on help-seeking for Korean ($\chi^2(1) = -.4099$, $p = .8744$), Vietnamese ($\chi^2(1) = 0.3618$, $p = .8596$, or Mexican ($\chi^2(1) = -.0406$, $p = .9838$) racial-ethnic heritage survivors, compared to European (White) survivors (Table 8).

These results contradict our second hypobook that shame is related to help-

seeking from informal support providers.

TABLE 8. Logistic Regression of Effects of Shame on Informal Help-Seeking With Moderation by Racial-Ethnic Group ($n = 182$)

Variable	Coefficient	SE	95% CI		p
			LL	UL	
Model Statistics: $\chi^2(7) = 4.30$, $p = .7447$ McFadden $R^2 = .0341$					
Shame (X)	.27	.60	-.90	1.45	.40
Korean (W1)[a]	-.41	2.59	-5.59	4.67	.87
Vietnamese (W2)[a]	-.36	2.05	-4.37	3.65	.86
Mexican (W3)[a]	-.04	2.01	-3.98	3.89	.98
Shame x Korean (XW1)[a]	.55	1.08	-1.56	2.66	.61
Shame x Vietnamese (XW2)[a]	.22	.81	-1.56	1.60	.98
Shame x Mexican (XW3)[a]	-.00	.76	-1.49	1.48	1.0
Shame x Ethnic Group (XW omnibus test): $\chi^2(3) = .35$, $p > .95$					

Note. CI = Confidence Interval; LL = lower limit;
UL = upper limit. [a]B = unstandardized beta
coefficient [b]Reference group: European (White)

Additionally, our third hypobook that racial-ethnic heritage would

moderate the association between shame and disclosure to informal sources

was also not significant $\chi^2(3) = .35$, $p > .95$, showing that the relationship

between shame and disclosure to informal support providers was not

moderated by racial-ethnic heritage (Figure 4).

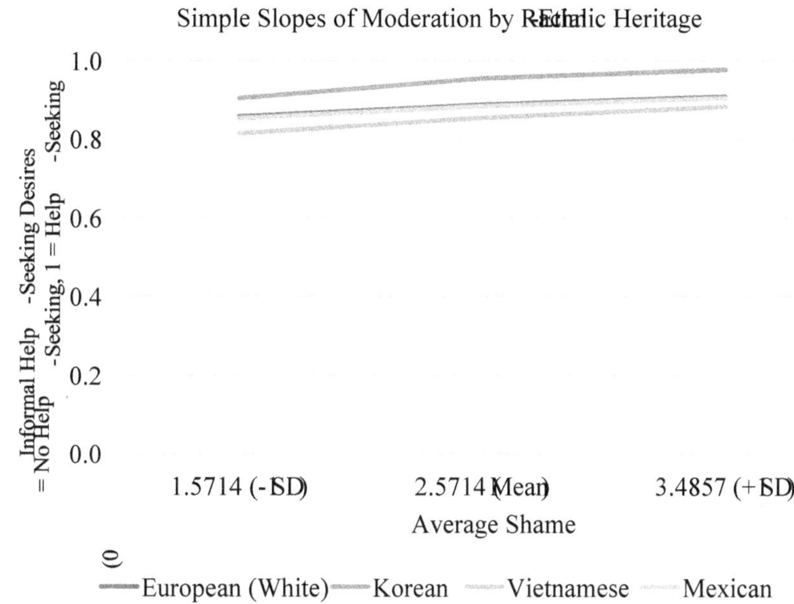

FIGURE 4. Simple slopes of moderation by racial-ethnic heritage for informal disclosure.

CHAPTER 4

DISCUSSION

The purpose of this study was to examine the role of shame and racial-ethnic heritage identity in predicting the nature and frequency of IPV survivors' help-seeking. The current study expanded on research about the impact of racial-ethnic heritage identity on help-seeking (Bridges et al., 2018; Monterrosa, 2021) as well as the influence of shame as a barrier to help-seeking (Crandall et al., 2005; McCleary-Sills et al., 2016). Previous literature surrounding help-seeking typically examined racial-ethnic heritage and help-seeking in isolation (Lipsky et al., 2006). In contrast, the current study included the emotional appraisal of shame as a factor when examining help-seeking desires.

For the first hypobook, we expected that racial-ethnic minority (Korean, Vietnamese, and Mexican) survivors of IPV would experience higher levels of shame than European (White) racial-ethnic heritage survivors. Contrary to researcher's expectations, there were no significant quantitative differences in average levels of shame between these four groups. This finding counters the current literature surrounding shame and racial-ethnic identity (Bent-Goodley, 2007), so researchers decided to examine individual questions on the TAQ to determine if racialethnic differences existed on specific items. When each question was individually examined, racial-ethnic heritage differences did emerge for three out of the seven TAQ shame subscale statements: "I felt embarrassed," "I felt

disgust," and "I felt humiliated."

Specifically, findings suggested that European (White) racial-ethnic

heritage survivors endorsed higher levels of embarrassment than Mexican

and Vietnamese racial-ethnic heritage survivors. Within IPV research,

embarrassment has been cited as a barrier to help-seeking for IPV survivors

in general (Krishnan et al., 2001; Sylaska & Edwards, 2014; Thaggard et

al., 2019). Including research that has suggested that racial-ethnic minority

survivors, like those of

Hispanic heritage, experience higher very high levels of embarrassment due

to IPV stigma (Bridges et al., 2018; Murdaugh et al., 2004; Rizo & Macy

2011). Although it is not clear why the current study found higher levels of

embarrassment amongst White survivors, a few studies have found that

individuals from racial-ethnic minority backgrounds report less

embarrassment about mental health issues than non-Hispanic White

participants (Diala et al., 2001; R. S. Shim et al., 2009). This raises the

possibility that there may, indeed, be important racial-ethnic differences in

feelings of embarrassment, but future empirical research around the feeling

of embarrassment amongst IPV survivors of different racial-ethnic

identities is needed to replicate this finding and further understand how

racial-ethnic heritage may impact feelings of embarrassment, in particular.

This study also found that European (White) racial-ethnic heritage survivors scored higher on the statement, "I felt disgust," than Mexican racial-ethnic heritage survivors. In terms of disgust, literature is non-existent for racial-ethnic heritage differences around feelings of disgust around IPV. Literature is abundant for feelings of guilt for IPV survivors (Beck et al., 2011; Overstreet & Quinn, 2013; Siegel et al., 2022), yet this does not capture feelings of personal disgust, especially for diverse survivors. However, the body image and personal body dissatisfaction literature has found higher levels of and negative body image and negative feelings among White women than women of color (Dye, 2016; Wildes et al., 2001). One qualitative study found that White women linked disgust to body dissatisfaction and fear of social rejection from others (Fahs, 2017).Differences in disgust between White women and women of color may stem from differences in individualism and collectivism. Literature on individualistic and collectivistic cultures show that people from Mexican, Vietnamese, and Korean racial-ethnic heritage backgrounds often come from collectivistic cultures (Ahrens et al.,

2010; Kennedy & Prock, 2018; Y. S. Lee & Hadeed, 2009; Y. Wong & Tsai, 2007) while

European (White) people in America are mostly raised in an individualistic culture (Fiske, 2002). Research on cultural differences between individualistic cultures and collectivistic cultures show that Americans report feeling more disengaging emotions, like disgust, than those from a collectivistic culture like Japan (Kitayama et al., 2006) which could explain why European (White) individuals in this study identified more with disgust than those from collectivistic cultures. Whether a similar dynamic is at play for IPV is worth considering for future research which needs to examine racial-ethnic differences in disengaging emotions like disgust.

Finally, the current study also found that both Mexican and European (White) racialethnic heritage survivors felt more humiliation than their Vietnamese counterparts. In cultures where family is emphasized, humiliation tactics are often used to keep the survivor from seeking help (Sabri et al., 2018). While this may explain why Mexican survivors may experience high levels of humiliation, it does not explain why European (White) survivors experience equally high levels of humiliation and why these levels are higher than Korean and Vietnamese survivors who also often have a strong familial orientation. While previous literature has examined racialethnic differences in shame more generally, the current study suggests that important differences may exist among different components of shame. Unfortunately, there is virtually no research on racial-ethnic differences in different components of shame such as embarrassment, humiliation, and disgust for IPV survivors. Future research is therefore needed to determine if and how different components of shame are experienced by IPV survivors of varying racial-ethnic backgrounds and why such differences might exist.

In contrast, none of the remaining TAQ shame items revealed any racial-ethnic differences. These remaining items on the TAQ shame subscale included feeling ashamed, losing sense of womanhood, feeling dirty inside, and that a shower could not wash away how dirty the participant felt. Contrary to previous research on ethnic differences in shame which has found that Mexican and Latinx survivors report higher levels of feeling dirty (Reina et al., 2014) and feeling ashamed (Murdaugh et al., 2004) after a sexual assault than survivors of other backgrounds, the current study did not detect any significant differences on these items. Similarly, previous research has also suggested that both Korean IPV survivors (Park et al., 2021) and Vietnamese IPV survivors (Bui, 2003) often report feeling ashamed as a barrier to help-seeking. One possible explanation of the lack of racial-ethnic differences in the current study is a lack of statistical variance. In the current study, ratings on items related to feeling ashamed and dirty were notably lower than ratings on items related to feeling embarrassed and humiliated. This could have resulted in a reduction in range, making it more difficult to detect racial-ethnic differences in these particular items. Future research is thus needed to determine whether some aspects of shame are experienced more often than others or whether the words used to assess shame carry different meanings or weight for survivors from different backgrounds.

One potential reason for our contradictory findings around shame could be that the items in the TAQ shame subscale all used first-person,

"I," statements which reflect an individualistic lexicon and sentence structure. While individualistic cultures place great emphasis on pride and individual achievement and failure (Eid & Diener, 2001), collectivistic cultures are more likely to experience pride based on the accomplishments and reputation of their families (Neumann et al., 2009). Unfortunately, the TAQ shame subscale questions were written from an individualistic perspective and do not include items that tap into the collective experience of shame. Future studies should thus utilize and include other shame scales to better examine shame in nested cultural context. Scales like the Interpersonal Shame Scale (ISS) were designed to examine various facets of shame within Asian American populations. Future studies should incorporate this scale to see if there are racial-ethnic differences in feelings of shame (Y. J. Wong et al., 2014). Also, the External and Internal Shame Scale (EISS) could be utilized to better understand interpersonal and intrapersonal shame for survivors of violence since the TAQ only examined interpersonal shame (Matos et al., 2023). This use of individualistic words instead of collectivistic words is not uncommon in American research over the past 50 years (Twenge et al., 2012), but it may be limiting our understanding of how people from different racial-ethnic backgrounds and cultures experience emotions such as shame. Our study found that being born in the U.S.A. and speaking English at home was positively correlated with higher average shame ratings. This could be due to the fact that individualistic words used in the U.S.A. are more focused on "I" statements like the TAQ. How we as researchers communicate and use language determines how participants will think about and answer our survey questions. Future researchers should thus expand on the TAQ shame subscale to include questions that examine collective shame to determine whether doing so would yield different results.

Another reason for the initial finding that shame did not differ based on a person's racialethnic heritage could be that shame is a universal emotion that can transcend different cultures which makes spotting racial-ethnic differences difficult (Tangney et al., 2005; Tracy & Matsumoto, 2008). In the context of IPV, the societal and cultural messages around shame for survivors of violence could be so strong that survivors from all cultures experiences shame, albeit in potentially different ways. Indeed, there could be a transcultural gendered effect around shame where women from all cultures are conditioned to feel shame around abuse, which makes it difficult to parse out specific racial-ethnic heritage differences. Literature has shown us that women from Mexican, Vietnamese, Korean, and European (White) racial-ethnic heritage backgrounds all feel shame (Mookerjee et al., 2015; Pham, 2014; Voth Schrag et al., 2021;Yang & Rosenblatt, 2001), and this was certainly true in the current study. Women from different cultures are taught to feel shame in patriarchal societies, and this pervasive sexism around female subordination transcends many cultures and racial-ethnic backgrounds (McCleary-Sills et al., 2016). In this way, shame is culturally and socially produced to silence survivors of violence, and women from different racial-ethnic backgrounds all experience shame around abuse and help-seeking.

However, how women experience shame may differ. For example, family and marriage are considered to be a core social institution in most cultures, but the pressure to maintain marriage or the lack of support for divorce can differ across cultures (Furtado et al., 2013). These cultural pressures to stay in a relationship may thus differ across racial-ethnic groups, which in turn can affect both shame and help-seeking. Future qualitative research is needed to examine how shame is experienced and its effects on informal and formal help-seeking. Unfortunately, this type of qualitative data was not captured in the current study. Future research should also examine other intersectional differences related to gender identity, religious beliefs, sexual identity and orientation, ability, military status, and other identities to determine how these identities intersect with racial-ethnic heritage to potentially affect the experience of shame and help-seeking in the context of female IPV survivors.

Understanding the role of sociodemographic variables is important because research on racial-ethnic group differences often comingles race-ethnicity with other socioeconomic differences such as income, occupation, education level, language usage, and others. Combining entire groups of people together into a simple racial-ethnic category is also problematic and runs the risk of reinforcing stereotypes. Indeed, researchers who study the model minority myth (Y. P. Kim & Lee, 2014; R. S. Shim et al., 2009) argue that these stereotypes often fail to capture diverse in-group differences. For example, the use of Confucian ideals to explain ethnic differences in behavior do not capture the experiences of all Asian people (Rošker, 2016). Similarly, the use of the category European/White in the current study may have missed important differences in this category, as well, as important cultural differences exist within European cultures and various religious identities (Bhopal & Donaldson, 1998). Furthermore, in a global world where different countries are available at the touch of a button and where global elite can move freely across borders, the simple racial-ethnic boxes we create as researchers cannot possibly capture the amalgamation of cultural influences affecting us all as more and more cultures mix and blur together. It is therefore paramount for future researchers to push against generalizations that one racial-ethnic heritage identity would act in a certain way and instead strive to learn about individual experiences within sociocultural contexts to fully understand how survivors of IPV experience shame and choose to seek help.

In addition to examining racial-ethnic differences in shame, the current study also examined differences in help-seeking among IPV survivors from different racial-ethnic backgrounds. In the current study, rates of overall help-seeking were exceptionally high (93.6%), and this was true of both informal help-seeking, and formal help-seeking. These findings are consistent with previous research which has found similarly high rates of overall disclosure (Brieding et al., 2014; Mahlstedt & Keeny, 1993);

however, our study did find a slightly higher rate of disclosure to both formal (73.2%) and informal (89%) support providers than previous research which found rates of disclosure to formal support providers that were closer to 60% (Ansara & Hindin, 2010; Barrett & Pierre, 2011) and rates of disclosure to informal support providers closer to 80% (Ansara & Hindin, 2010; Mahlstedt & Keeny, 1993).

One reason for the higher rates of help-seeking found in this study could be the way that participants were recruited. The data from this study was pulled from a larger study that gathered data on diverse racial-ethnic heritage survivors of violence within the past five years. Researchers used adaptive sampling (R. Campbell et al., 2004; S. K. Thompson, 1997) techniques by focusing recruitment efforts at known community spaces, like social service organizations and neighborhood events, where researchers felt that female-identified survivors of Mexican, Korean, Vietnamese, and European (White) racial-ethnic heritage identities might frequent. This sampling technique could have influenced our high help-seeking results due to the fact that most people who attend these events are seeking help for something from social programs or looking for community support. Since participants for this study heard about this study through direct outreach, they self-selected into this study as opposed to other studies that use a random sample of a specific population, and these differences in recruitment method could have influenced our help-seeking findings. This possibility is reflected in the fact that over 40% of Korean participants had sought help from an advocate, and one of our recruitment

sites was a domestic violence organization that provides culturally specific

services to Asian and Pacific Islander populations.

Similarly, the fact that the Southern California area has large and highly
established

Mexican, Korean, and Vietnamese communities may have enabled higher

rates of help-seeking. Research suggests that cultural and language barriers

may deter help-seeking among these groups in other areas of the country

(Silva-Martínez, 2016), but large ethnic populations in Southern California

mean that there are a variety of formal services that offer culturally

grounded and competent services in the language of our target groups and

provided by people within their community, which may have made help-

seeking easier for IPV survivors in Los Angeles County and Orange

County than it is in other parts of the country. Future research should

compare participants from Mexican, Korean, and Vietnamese IPV

survivors from various parts of the U.S.A.

Although overall help-seeking was high, the current study did not

find any significant differences in rates overall or informal among survivors

from different racial-ethnic backgrounds. However, there were differences

in formal help-seeking. Specifically, Vietnamese survivors were less likely

to seek help from formal support providers, the main effect of raceethnicity

on help-seeking was not significant in our larger moderated linear

regressions suggesting that the role of racial-ethnic heritage in predicting formal help-seeking is less influential when other variables are included in the model. Being a European (White) woman in America affords some survivors more privileges than racial-ethnic minority survivors, and ethnic minority survivors face many barriers due to a lack of knowledge of available resources and experiences of discrimination (Hulley et al., 2023).

Although differences in overall help-seeking did not emerge in the current study, there were some significant differences by type of support provider (Table 3). Specifically, around half of Mexican and European (White) survivors sought help from formal entities like police and counselors or mental health professionals. One reason for this finding could be that as severity of abuse increased, help-seeking to certain formal outlets that can help with psychological abuse, like counselors, or physical interventions, like police, would be necessary as severity of abuse increased. Correlations between shame and type of abuse showed that physical and sexual abuse were positively correlated with higher average levels of shame. This is consistent with previous research that shows that help-seeking increases as severity of abuse increases (Duterte et al., 2008); however, neither sexual, physical, nor psychological abuse were significantly related to help-seeking when included as covariates in our larger moderated linear regression model, suggesting that the role these variables played in help-seeking is less important than other variables.

Mexican IPV survivors were also the most likely out of any racial-ethnic heritage background to seek help from their own family. One reason for this finding is that there is a cultural pressure to not bring shame or scrutiny upon the family by disclosing to outside sources. As a result, Mexican IPV survivors might instead prefer to seek help from their family. This is consistent with IPV literature where Mexican racial-ethnic heritage survivors do not seek help from external outlets like formal entities because violence should be kept within the family (Bauer et al., 2000; Rizo & Macy, 2011). Future qualitative research is needed to better understand why survivors from different racial-ethnic backgrounds choose formal or informal help-seeking options.

The comparatively low rates of help-seeking among our Vietnamese survivors are also noteworthy. With the exception of informal disclosures, Vietnamese survivors had lower rates of disclosure to every other type of support provider. There are several possible explanations of this finding. First, the Vietnamese population has a very different pattern of immigration than Korean and Mexican immigrants. Post-Vietnam war, there was a large increase in Vietnamese immigrants to the United States who are a comparatively new addition to American society (Kula et al., 2021). Many Vietnamese immigrants wanted to escape their communist government and came to America with very little education compared to other immigrants coming to

America (Rumbaut, 2000). Racism, language barriers, and U.S.A. culture made it difficult for

Vietnamese to assimilate into the new country (Kula et al., 2021). Indeed sample data from the

2022 American community survey suggests that, consistent with our study, VietnameseAmericans tend to have less education, lower household incomes, and are less likely to speak English than their Korean-American counterparts (U.S. Census Bureau, 2021). As a result, Vietnamese immigrants might be less familiar with services or experience more language barriers compared to the Korean population in the United States.

Alternatively, the lower rates of help-seeking we found among Vietnamese survivors in our sample may have resulted from differences in relationship patterns. In our study, a substantial number of our Vietnamese participants were still in a relationship with their abusive partner (60%). Literature around shame appraisals tells a slightly different story than what we found in this study: survivors who have lower levels of shame predicted readiness to leave a relationship one year later whereas our study found that low levels of shame in Vietnamese IPV survivors meant that they would be more likely to still be in a relationship with their abuser (Matlow & DePrince, 2015). It is possible that survivors who remain in their abusive relationship may be less likely to acknowledge shame because they have not yet acknowledged that something in their relationship is not right. The desire to stay in the relationship and not ruin a current family dynamic has been linked to less help seeking (Dziegielewski, et al., 2005), and research suggests that there are many barriers to seeking help like not wanting to hurt their family or culture barriers to leaving relationships (O'Doherty et al., 2016). It is possible that these pressures may be greater for survivors of Vietnamese descent, leading them to stay in abusive relationships rather than seek help. Research around IPV survivors still with their abusive partner shows that there are many barriers to seeking help like not wanting to hurt or shame their family and culture due to the familial expectations around IPV that prohibits a survivor from leaving their abusive partner (O'Doherty et al., 2016). It is possible that a person would experience more shame or acknowledge shame and be more likely to seek help when they are ready to leave their partner or after they leave a partner. Future research should therefore further examine the role of staying in the abusive relationship on shame, help-seeking, and the relationship between these variables among different racial-ethnic groups.

Contrary to our predictions, higher levels of shame were not related to lower helpseeking. This contradicts previous research that has found that shame is a barrier to help-seeking (Beaulaurier et al., 2005; Petersen et al., 2005;). One potential reason for this nonsignificant finding may be that help-seeking was overall extremely high in the current study. With nearly all survivors disclosing to at least one person, there simply may not have been enough variance to predict differences. Future research is therefore needed with a larger sample that includes survivors who both did and did not disclose to others to determine the potential role of shame and racial-ethnic heritage. Further examination is also needed to understand the multitude of situational factors not captured in the current study that might affect survivors' help-seeking (Sylaska & Edwards, 2014). For example, literature around disclosures and help-seeking shows that survivors are more likely to seek help if they feel supported (Catallo et al., 2012) and not judged for their IPV experience (Feder et al., 2006). Future research should aim to capture these situational factors to provide a more holistic and well-rounded picture of facilitators and barriers to disclosure for informal or formal options.

More variance in help-seeking would also be needed to accurately detect the potential moderating effect of racial-ethnic heritage on the relationship between shame and help-seeking.
The only analysis to show any statistical significance involved formal help-seeking as the outcome. Notably, formal help-seeking had the most variance overall with only 73.7% of survivors in the sample having disclosed to a formal support provider. With nearly all participants disclosing to at least one person (93.6%), differences in slopes across four ethnic groups may simply have been impossible to statistically detect in our overall help-seeking model (Table 4). Future research with larger and more varied samples is thus needed to further examine the potentially moderating role of race-ethnicity on the relationship between shame and helpseeking.

Nonetheless, this study did find that Korean survivors were more likely to use formal entities as their average levels of shame increased, but this relationship between shame and formal help-seeking did not exist for any of the other racial-ethnic heritage groups in this study. This suggests that for most survivors in this sample, there was no relationship between shame help-seeking, but there was a relationship between shame and formal help-seeking for survivors of Korean descent. Why this is so is difficult to explain due to the underdeveloped literature on why Korean survivors of IPV go to formal entities. This question therefore deserves attention in future studies. One possible explanation is that Korean IPV survivors may have experienced higher levels of abuse which functioned as a lurking variable that was related to both shame and help-seeking. Although prior literature has shown that help-seeking increases as severity of types of abuse increases (Lelaurain et al., 2017), neither psychological, sexual, nor physical abuse were significantly related to help-seeking when used as covariates in the current study, suggesting that the lurking variable hypobook is not true. It is also possible that Korean IPV survivors may have felt more comfortable utilizing formal resources because of their significantly higher education levels, and it is possible that education level could affect the relationship between shame and help-seeking. Future research should therefore examine this question further through qualitative and quantitative interviews. Prior literature shows us that IPV survivors who have higher levels of education are more likely to utilize formal help-seeking options like mental health professionals than women with less education (Kaukinen et al., 2013). It is possible that survivors with higher education like our Korean survivors were more likely to seek help from formal entities and the shame they experienced was a result of trying to seek help.

Indeed, it is possible that help-seeking might lead to shame instead of shame leading to help-seeking. In the current study, we hypothesized that higher levels of shame would lead to lower levels of help-seeking, but it is equally possible that negative experiences during helpseeking, particularly with formal providers such as the police, might lead to higher feelings of shame. This could help explain the positive relationship between shame and formal help-seeking that was found for our Korean heritage survivors. One possibility is that Korean IPV survivors in this study experienced more negative reactions during their formal help-seeking which could have led to higher levels of average shame. Prior literature has shown that if a survivor has a negative experience when seeking help from informal outlets or various personal networks, formal help-seeking will be utilized (Macy et al., 2005). Unfortunately, the nature and quality of formal reactions to IPV survivor help-seeking was not examined in the current study, but prior literature has shown that survivors of color do receive more negative reactions from formal support providers like the police (Decker et al., 2019). These negative reactions may have resulted in higher levels of average shame for Korean heritage IPV survivors. Among Korean survivors, in particular, negative reactions related to language misunderstandings or differences are not uncommon and can act as a barrier to help-seeking (R. S. Shim et al., 2009). It is also possible that differences in which formal support providers survivors disclosed to may have played a role. Notably, Korean survivors had the highest rate of disclosure to religious personnel.

Based on prior literature, many Korean Americans are associated with some type of religion (I. J. Kim et al., 2006; Ley, 2008), and a long history of Christian missionary work in South Korea has resulted in high levels of Christianity among Korean heritage people living in the U.S.A. (R. Y. Kim, 2017). One possible explanation of the positive relationship between shame and formal help-seeking among Korean survivors may thus be that religious personnel are more likely to react negatively or more likely to minimize a survivor's experience which then leads to higher levels of shame due to religious pressure from leaders or members of the congregation. Similarly, religiosity itself might affect and mold how survivors think about abuse, shame, helpseeking, and the importance of marriage or staying with a partner. Although there was not a religiosity measure in the current study, future studies should examine the relationship between religiosity and shame among IPV survivors from all cultures.

The relationship between shame and formal help-seeking for Korean women could also be affected by expectations. Korean-Americans have a longer history of immigration to the United States than most Vietnamese and many Mexican immigrants. Many Korean-Americans immigrated to the United States after the Korean War (Baik, 2019; Xiaojian, 2016) while many Vietnamese and Mexican immigrants have arrived more recently. As a result of immigration patterns, Korean survivors might be more similar to European (White) populations in their helpseeking patterns and their expectations of the type of help they expect to receive. Korean survivors may have also had less shame to start with because of their relatively high social capital which may have led them to reach out for help to formal services with the expectation of receiving help regardless of their racial-ethnic identity. If these IPV survivors were instead met with negative and/or racist reactions, the experiences may have been particularly shameful because it was less expected than it may have been for Mexican and Vietnamese survivors.

Unfortunately, the current study did not include an acculturation measure or measures of disclosure expectations which could test these hypotheses. Future longitudinal research should thus examine the role of acculturation through both quantitative and qualitative approaches to examine how a survivor feels shame and if negative or positive help-seeking reactions lead to more or less shame over time.

Limitations

Significant limitations in study methodology and design may have affected our ability to detect relationships between shame and help-seeking and the interaction between shame and racial-ethnic identity on help-seeking desires for survivors of IPV. To begin, data were collected cross-sectionally and not longitudinally. The statements posed to participants to assess their feelings of shame were part of the TAQ shame subscale, which participants would then rate on a scale of 1 (strongly disagree) to 5 (strongly agree) at one specific point in time (DePrince et al., 2010). The feelings of shame when survivors took this survey might not accurately represent the same feelings about shame when they decided to seek help. Trajectory research on depression and PTSD shows that over time depression often decreases after an assault (Feiring et al., 2002). For emotions like shame, research shows that shame has been shown to dissipate over time (De Rubeis & Hollenstein, 2009; Goffnett et al., 2020). Future research should examine Also, the current study hypothesized that higher levels of shame would lead to lower levels of helpseeking where shame would have been interpreted as a barrier to help-seeking, researchers would have wanted to examine the direction of effects; that is, if shame affects help-seeking or if helpseeking affects shame, or if effects are bidirectional. It is also possible that what occurred when survivors disclosed lead to shame or that there is a circular effect with each other acting the other in an iterative way. The cross-sectional nature of the data precluded assumptions about directionality. Future research should examine shame longitudinally, not cross-sectionally, to examine if IPV survivors experience a decrease in shame as time progresses.

Most literature has assumed a negative relationship between shame and help-seeking, where higher levels of shame make help-seeking less likely (McCleary-Sills et al., 2016; Thaggard & Montayre, 2019). However, it is also possible that lower levels of shame may lead to higher levels of help-seeking. A negative relationship between shame and help-seeking could suggest that survivors with higher levels of shame were less likely to reach out for help, but it could also suggest that people who sought out help had lower levels of shame because helpseeking served as an antidote to shame. According to Brown's (2006) theory of shame resilience, positive help-seeking experiences may be an antidote to shame. The theory of shame resilience suggests that there are four steps to resisting the negative effects of shame: (1) the person first needs to recognize when they are experiencing shame, (2) the person then needs to critically evaluate what is driving their shame, (3) the person then needs to reach out to others and practice help-seeking, and finally, (4) the person should talk about how they are feeling and ask for what they need. What this theory suggests is that shame thrives in silence. To overcome the toxic effects of shame, people need to talk about their feelings of shame and experience empathy from supportive others (Brown, 2006). In this way, shame is not just a barrier to help-seeking; helpseeking may also serve as a remedy for shame when support providers respond in an empathetic and supportive way. This could potentially show researchers more about the findings in the current study since a large number of participants did seek help from some formal or informal. Future research on shame for survivors of IPV can examine this question longitudinally so that researchers can make conclusions about the temporal relationship between shame and helpseeking.

Additionally, although the TAQ shame subscale measure did ask participants to rate their feelings of shame after the assault, rating emotions retrospectively is not as valid as assessing emotional experiences at the time they were experienced. This study focused on survivor's experience of IPV within the past 5 years. If a survivor recently experienced violence, their emotions like shame might be heightened as opposed to a survivor recalling a violent experience that happened further in the past. Therefore, future research should aim to examine this relationship in a longitudinal framework instead of a cross-sectional approach. Also, the TAQ shame subscale was specifically created for sexual assault and not for IPV. Even though it was tested on a diverse group of people, it was also not written to understand shame in Asian populations. Had this subscale been designed for Asian populations the potential way that the questions were asked could have been different, tying in familial shame as well as cultural shame.

Another limitation of this study was the issue utilizing dichotomous variables for helpseeking. This study wanted to know if participants disclosed their experiences with violence to formal or informal help-seeking options. Quantitative data for this study was able to understand some of the formal and informal outlets, but there are many more options help-seeking options like a professor or a human resource officer that may have slipped through the cracks due to the limited amount of questions about help-seeking options. Even though this study was able to better understand some help-seeking decisions, more nuanced help-seeking options were not captured due to the yes/no questions that were asked. In the future, researchers should allow space for participants to qualitatively answer questions about who they sought help from so that researchers can find out what type of formal or informal outlet was used but they can also get a better sense of how many people a person sought help from in their own words.

Strengths

Despite these limitations, the current study has several strengths. To begin, traditional psychological research lacks sample diversity (Henrich et al., 2010). This means that marginalized people often are not researched or included within specific sample populations as researchers typically utilize college students for their studies. Most of the time these college students are not representative of the general population and results often provide a very limited scope of what is possibly generalizable to the public (Henrich et al., 2010). To address this problem, we recruited a diverse sample of participants outside of a college campus and within the surrounding community. These target ethnicities were chosen because of the large population of Mexican, Korean, Vietnamese, and European (White) racial-ethnic heritage people in both Los Angeles and Orange Counties. Across the United States, these racial-ethnic heritage populations are quickly growing. Representing diversity in this study was a priority to the researchers in order to explore how people of different racial-ethnic backgrounds process and seek help from IPV. Also, the reliability of the shame subscale for the TAQ used for this study was extremely high (α = .91), further proving the validity of the TAQ and its reliability across various populations and samples. These strengths show the benefits of diverse sample recruitment and amplifies the validity and reliability of a developed questionnaire.

Future Implications

Understanding and adhering to survivor needs after a violent incident is and should be of the utmost importance to researchers and service care providers. Often, survivors who are seeking help are given mainstream interventions that fail to incorporate their cultural and racialethnic backgrounds into their support and treatment. Incorporating intersectional frameworks to survivor advocacy and support, by furthering our understanding of emotional appraisals and racial-ethnic experiences may push these survivor-centered approaches to more mainstream practices and provide opportunities for both formal and informal care providers to utilize culturally competent approaches when working with survivors (Kulkarni, 2019). This is important because many services given to survivors of IPV were developed based on a European-white American culture and not developed from a diverse cultural lens (Rodríguez et al., 2009; U.S. Department of Health and Human Services, 2001). Rather than administering generalized programs that are assumed to work for all survivors, providers should consider an individualized care plan that supports survivors' unique needs and experiences while incorporating a survivor's racial-ethnic heritage and background. Further, the integration of a person's ethnicity into their specific care program is often underdeveloped (Watt et al., 2016). Prior research findings have shown that integrating a person's culture and ethnicity into their individualized care plan can reap a plethora of positive outcomes and benefits for the survivor like a reduction in the feeling of shame, regaining their dignity, and experiencing hope (Allen & Wozniak, 2011; McGoldrick et al., 2005).

Another goal of this study is to support holistic care for IPV survivors. When survivors are given resources, these resources are only one piece of a larger puzzle within survivor advocacy (McLeod et al., 2010). This study proves the importance of self-awareness and emotional appraisals. Service care providers can use emotional appraisals to validate and assist the clients they work with (McLeod et al., 2010). The one-size-fits-all approach can have detrimental consequences for IPV survivors; researchers and service care providers need to consider the multidimensional characteristics of humans to provide the best help. Our goal as researchers is to promote holistic approaches to service care provision so that survivors have more tools at their disposal to heal from their experience with IPV. Information about the role of culture and shame on survivor help-seeking can help push forward intersectional frameworks in developing and implementing survivor advocacy and support, leading to more culturally appropriate and nuanced services for survivors (Kulkarni, 2019).

Findings of the current study also have important implications for community education around shame, stigma, and help-seeking for formal or informal service care providers. Survivors of IPV often experience shame (Beck et al., 2015; Deitz et al., 2015) and feel stigma (Overstreet & Quinn, 2013; Williams & Mickelson, 2008) around their violent experience which can cause survivors to not seek help from professionals. A lack of IPV training within formal support systems, like police and medical personnel, involving shame and stigma as barriers to helpseeking fail to holistically support IPV survivors. In order to break down the intrapersonal and interpersonal barriers like shame and stigma, community and formal help-seeking options need to bring awareness and educate themselves and the public on these barriers (Sylaska & Edwards, 2014). At a minimum, this training for formal help-seeking options should focus on the experience of shame and stigma around help-seeking which then can be brough to informal providers as an educational program. Not only can service providers act as educators around these barriers, but these entities can also reinforce shame due to lack of knowledge on survivor healing (Crowe & Murray, 2015). These providers, knowingly or unknowingly, can aggravate survivor fears of being shamed by those in positions of power or family members which can halt the help-seeking process. Community organizations and formal help-seeking options can use the findings of this study to train other formal support providers on how to tackle difficult discussions around racial-ethnic heritage, shame, stigma, and help-seeking opportunities to support survivors of IPV. These trainings can then be brought to all community members so that informal support systems, like friends and family, can also combat shame and stigma around help-seeking. Together, this research can provide a more holistic view of a survivor and bring awareness to the experience of shame and racial-ethnic heritage as it relates to help-seeking options.

www.ingramcontent.com/pod-product-compliance
Lightning Source LLC
LaVergne TN
LVHW011304210726
843509LV00016B/785